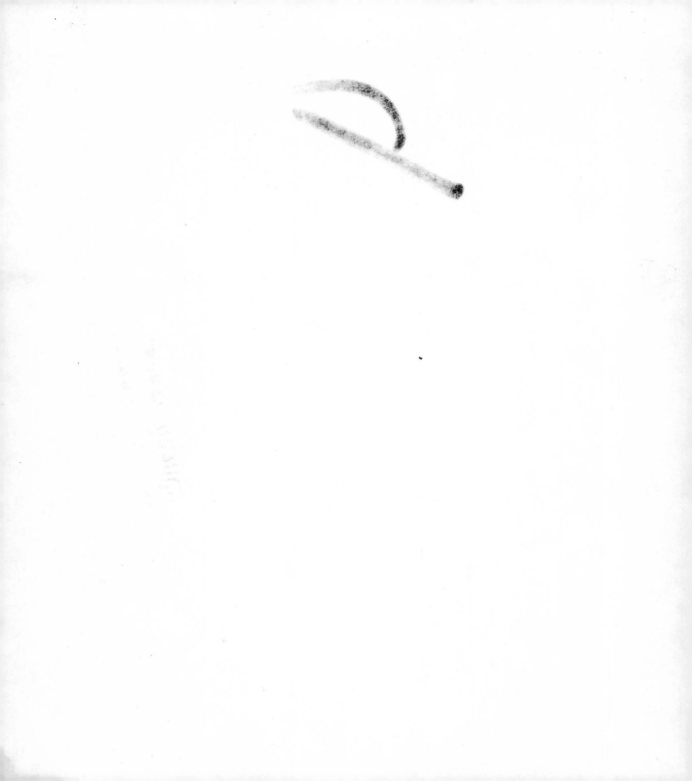

Romain Goldron

ANCIENT AND ORIENTAL MUSIC

H. S. Stuttman Company, Inc., Publishers
Distributed by Doubleday & Company, Inc.

Designed by Erik Nitsche

Copyright © 1968 H. S. Stuttman Co., Inc.
All rights reserved
Copyright © 1966 Editions Rencontre

#
HISTORY
OF
MUSIC
♭

1

1 Wooden drum decorated with human masks.
(Bamoum region, Cameroon)
2 Idiophone, a percussion instrument. (Benin, Nigeria)
3 Sanza, a type of idiophone. (Central Africa)
4 Stringed instrument. (Isle of Timor, Indonesia)
5 Triple musical bow. (New Guinea)
6 Sheng, a Chinese mouth organ.
7 Harp in the shape of a human body. (Africa)
8 Sistrum, a frame rattle. (Mali)

4

8

Contents

9

10

11

12

13

9 *Harpist. (Ancient Greece)*
10 *Man from the Upper Volta playing
the musical bow.*
11 *Flute players from Turkestan.*
12 *Muse playing the lyre. (Etruscan art—
5th century B.C.)*
13 *Chinese flute seller.*

INTRODUCTION

A critic asserted recently that the time has passed
when any one author could claim to have mastered
a subject as vast as the history of music. The future lay in collective studies by specialist contribu-
tors.

Nowadays all branches of learning, including
musicology, depend increasingly on specialists;
thanks to their invaluable research, much previously unknown or underrated music has become
accessible to us. We have only to consider the
growing popularity of medieval music to realize
the change of attitude that has taken place in the
last hundred years or so. Without dwelling on
Victor Hugo's firm belief that music began with
Palestrina in the 16th century, we should read
the pages devoted to the Notre Dame School of
composers (*ca.* 1150-1220), or to Guillaume de
Machaut (*ca.* 1300-1377), in books written by
music historians early this century. Their incom-
prehension makes us smile, now that we have easy
access to recordings of the music of these composers.

The task of preparing medieval music for the
concert platform or recording studio is detailed

and arduous. It involves deciphering the texts and signs, transcribing the music into modern notation, and studying contemporary documents to discover the authentic style of performance. We are indebted to the patient teamwork of research scholars for the lively renderings we hear today of music that until comparatively recently was dismissed as primitive and crude.

Despite this emphasis on specialization, however, it may be argued that there is still a need for a synthesis of ideas. All too often today the layman feels out of his depth when confronted with the bewildering amount of new knowledge at his disposal. A distinction must be drawn between the kind of material necessary for the specialist and that suitable for the educated and interested amateur. There is room for an informative work that avoids dry scholarship without resorting to oversimplification. This I have attempted to achieve.

The progress in color printing has enabled us to present the reader with lavish illustrations. Besides being a delight to the eye, they complement the aims of the text. They bring the layman nearer to the styles of life and art of the past, and in so doing help him to discover the unique beauty of the music of a particular period.

The presence of these rich illustrations, taken from authentic documents, encouraged me to compare music with the visual arts, whenever the occasion arose. After all, do not all the diverse manifestations of an epoch stem from the same soil and draw their inspiration from the same dreams? Almost simultaneously, the same aspirations haunt the spirits of poets, philosophers, architects and musicians in a given era, in spite of apparent—and often revealing—external differences.

I have taken this idea a step further. I have endeavored to set music in the environment from which it sprang. From whence did musicians draw their resources? For whom did they write? How did they set about composing? Who played their works? These are some of the questions I have tried to answer.

My aim being to give a many-sided picture of the history of music, I have not hesitated to use quotations from the works of certain authors who have brought new and illuminating ideas to the subject. Needless to say, the sources are always indicated, either in the text or in the notes at the end of the volume.

R. G.

Prehistoric music
Its survival from ancient to modern times
The mythological and sacred origins
of music and instruments

Forty Thousand Years Ago . . .

Music occupies a unique place in the arts. Although its practice dates from prehistoric times, it was not written down until very much later. Furthermore, the concept of musical composition, as it was developed in the West in the Christian era, originated a mere few centuries ago. The use that our particular civilization has made of the art of sound, the increasingly complex tonal constructions it has created for its enlightenment or simply for its pleasure, are sufficient alone to distinguish it from all other civilizations.

On the other hand, many masterpieces of poetry, painting and architecture have survived from remotest antiquity, which in their beauty and technical perfection bear testimony to a high spiritual and artistic level of development. The civilizations that conceived them are dead, and yet live on in their works.

This is completely untrue of music, even though the earliest known document relating to music is estimated to be no less than forty thousand years old! This document actually consists of a series of wall paintings in a grotto at Trois Frères in Ariège (southern France). These extraordinary paintings depict a primitive musical instrument. The instrument is the musical bow.

15

A New Science: Musical Ethnography

Nothing seems more capricious than the path of history; it is fraught with unexpected twists and gaps. Peoples, cultures and civilizations, apparently destined for the heights, suddenly become arid, mysteriously losing their powers of invention and creation. They merely survive, without making the slightest attempt to increase their knowledge; for centuries on end they are quite content to reiterate tirelessly and with blind devotion the learning of their ancestors. But such abruptly stunted growth is an invaluable source of study for the historian. These forgotten and abandoned peoples, who continue with superstitious respect to repeat the ways and customs of their forefathers—far from the theatre of life where human destiny plays its part— are living monuments of the distant past. In these societies, which have in some cases lapsed into an almost primitive state, prehistory has survived right to the threshold of our technological age. Indeed, it seems all too likely that such present-day amenities as television and radio, phonograph and motion picture, will soon destroy these last vestiges of our origins.

In recent years, combined research projects in archaeology, history, ethnography and musicology have greatly widened and deepened our vision of the history of music. The scientific study of folklore and popular song has revealed ancient musical structures in modern guise. It has been possible to correlate these in turn with the vocal and instrumental traditions of the Orient, and with those of primitive tribes whose geographical location has protected them from any real contact with the modern world.

Summing up, then, we find ourselves in rather a paradoxical position. On the one hand, scientific research has bewildered us by revealing a musical tradition forty thousand years old; on the other, it has shown that the distant past continues to exist only a few hours away by air from our big capital cities, in regions curiously impervious to progress: in Africa, Australia, Siberia, the South Sea Islands, Central Asia, and—if one removes the modern veneer—in the songs and airs of Europe. We do not need a great deal of research to find examples in the songs and airs of the people, for example, in Brittany and the Balkans, Finland and Spain, or in the remote valleys of the Swiss Alps.

It is not altogether fanciful, then, to ask ourselves what role music played in the lives of our Stone Age ancestors of the Paleolithic and Neolithic periods. What is more, it is possible for us to know what it sounded like.[1]

10

15 *Mythological scene. Man disguised as a bison playing a musical bow and marking time, preceded by two animals, one half-stag, half-bison, and the other a reindeer with webbed forefeet (Middle Magdalenian Culture—grotto of Trois-Frères, Ariège)*
16 *Harp-kithara made of bark.* (The Origin of Musical Instruments *by A. Schaeffner, Paris, 1936*)

16

In the Beginning Was Sound . . .

If the exact significance of Paleolithic art and sculpture remains something of an enigma, one thing at least is fairly certain: the moving force behind their creation was essentially the same as that which inspired such artists as Giotto (*ca.* 1267-1337) or the Indian, d'Adjouta, to cover the walls of a Christian church or a Hindu temple with frescoes. The stimulus was of a sacred or supernatural order.

The mask worn by the musician depicted in the grotto at Trois-Frères leaves us in little doubt as to his magical or ritualistic function. Disguised in an animal skin, he is playing a musical bow, an instrument still in use among certain primitive tribes, notably the African Bochimans; the sound of the instrument seems to be having a hypnotic effect on the two reindeer (or reindeer and bison) in front of him. (One cannot help seeing him as a primitive incarnation of Orpheus, possessed with the additional mystical powers of the Siberian shamans.)

In a later wall painting, discovered in Southeast Africa, four women are shown, all playing musical bows and apparently taking part in some rite. Despite their stylized postures, their slim silhouettes form astonishingly graceful arabesques, which could suggest that these musicians were also dancers.

We have proof, then, that the practice of music existed as early as the Paleolithic Age. How important was its role? Since the recent fruitful researches of Marius Schneider, we may answer categorically that music played a central part in the life of prehistoric man.[2] Having made a detailed study of the myths, legends and beliefs of the age, Schneider was struck by the fact that even the most primitive peoples were familiar with the concept that sound forms the basis of reality in the universe. "Whenever the genesis of the world is described with due regard for detail, an acoustic element intervenes at the decisive moment of action. Every time a god carries out his will to make himself or another god manifest, or to create the sky, the earth, or man, he utters a sound. He will sigh, gasp, speak, sing, roar, cough, spit, hiccough, vomit, thunder, or—play a musical instrument."

The source from which the world springs is essentially acoustic: "The primeval abyss is, then, a fount of resonance, and the sound which issues from it must be considered as the primary creative force, generally personified in mythology by the god-singers. The representation of these gods . . . in the form of a musician, an echoing cavern in the rocks, or a head (be it human or animal) uttering a cry, is clearly nothing but a concession to the pictorial language of mythology."[3]

We realize at once how important the place of music is with primitive tribes whose religious beliefs are expressed by way of ritualistic ceremonies. Through the medium of music men strive to emulate their gods, or, by rites and incantations, to evoke the sacred moment of creation. The powers of a magician, a priest, or a shaman are contained in his voice or "in some supernatural device which, ultimately, is always a musical instrument or a symbol of sound."[4]

Another result of the cosmic function accorded to music is that the musician finds himself in a central and exalted position, due to his mystical communion with the spirits and souls of the dead.

It is hardly necessary to add that this is still the case today among certain primitive peoples. Marcea Eliade has emphasized the essential role that music plays for the shaman or medicine man in his preparations for a state of trance.[5]

The Magic Power of Musical Instruments

It goes without saying that in such a context musical instruments cannot be regarded as commonplace, functional objects. As Marius Schneider puts it: "Every musical instrument forms a focal point for society. It is the altar on which are sacrificed the utterances of the gods."[6] It is hardly surprising, therefore, that instruments are treated with respect, and that their shapes are governed by the dictates of mythology rather than by the laws of acoustics.

Still today we see examples among certain tribes of a naive veneration for their musical instruments. The Bayankole people make daily offerings of milk to their royal drums, which, they believe, represent sacred cows; the Hindus (Pura-Nannuru) also treat the drum as though it were a god, taking infinite care to wash and perfume it each day, and to lay it reverently on a couch.[7]

Our modern Western society is by no means lacking in examples of the magic powers of musical instruments. Think of the legends that so rapidly surrounded the figure of Paganini and his "diabolical" virtuosity; his violin, like the one in Stravinsky's *The Soldier's Tale,* left in its wake the deathly smell of brimstone.

Further instances crowd to mind, from Mozart's *The Magic Flute* to E.T.A. Hoffmann's *Violin of Cremona;* from the Pied Piper of Hamelin to the enchanted harps whose strings vibrate of their own accord; and finally, of course, the wondrous horns which sound right across the literature and music of the Romantic era. Many folk legends perpetuate in our libraries and concert-halls the bewitching

17

18

19

20 *Bone flutes, decorated with feathers from*
Amazonian parrots and the wings of Coleoptera beetles.
(Orinoco Basin, Venezuela)

powers of musical instruments! We must remember too that in Germany, until the beginning of the 18th century, the horn, that supreme symbol of sorcery, remained suspect in the eyes of the religious and civil authorities. (Its spellbinding qualities are exploited even today in the hunt.) As late as 1711 a princely decree forbade the horn to be played other than at certain court functions. While brass instruments such as trombones, clarinos and trumpets enjoyed considerable popularity, the horn was not admitted into German town bands until the time of J. S. Bach.[8]

We, with our modern, practical outlook on life, are astonished to discover that the musical bow preceded that used for archery. "Musical instruments were constructed first, and only later transformed into implements, whose power stemmed from their musical origins. The musical bow led to the bow and arrow, the horn was adopted for signaling purposes, the flute inspired the idea of bellows, the harp suggested the shape of a boat, and the drum formed the outline of a wheel, or even of a chariot."[9]

It is, then, against this background of sacred and superstitious beliefs that we must view the scenes painted in the grottos of prehistory and the ceremonies they represent. It seems probable that in these rites each person had a precise, predeter-mined function; this, indeed, is true of all traditional societies except our own Western culture. Gilbert Rouget sums up this idea neatly as follows: "It is always a certain kind of person who plays a certain type of instrument in a certain sort of situation, sometimes in only a certain place, in the presence of certain specific people at certain events which could occur only very rarely."[10]

Did Polyphony Exist in the Paleolithic Age?

Besides the musical bow, other instruments in use in the Upper Paleolithic period were the flute, drum and horn, the latter being made of wood, animal horn or ivory. According to the musicologist André Schaeffner, it is not certain whether the horn appeared before or after the flute and whistle, but all three definitely preceded the musical bow. An interesting find on the Paleolithic site of the Dordogne was an instrument linking music and magic. It is a kind of Stone Age planchette, a revolving wooden board in the shape of a rhombus, "the hum of which," states Schaeffner, "was supposed to represent the voices of the spirits."

It is generally accepted that melodies based on specific note-groups or scales (e.g., the pentatonic scale) must have existed since the Paleolithic Age[11]; it seems also that there may have been some

21

22

simple form of polyphony, judging from the important role this plays in the music of present-day primitive races, such as the African and Malaccan Pgymies and the Bochimans. "Each player reiterates a short melodic phrase which, entwined with others, forms a richly-textured and continuous flow of sound";[12] interjected cries and rhythmic hand-clapping and foot-stamping complete the effect. Walter Wiora sees in this method of combining voices a rudimentary form of the faux-bourdon and canon, which developed in the Middle Ages.

Not only are there striking similarities between the life and art of the distant past and that of primitive tribes today, but also between these tribes themselves. The music of the Pygmies, for instance, bears a close resemblance to that of certain tribes in Lapland and Siberia, despite their geographic isolation; this is true also of the music of the Papous and of small primitive communities in Australia, Ceylon and Tierra del Fuego.

With the passing of the Paleothic, the Neolithic Age brought the development of agriculture and consequently more settled communities, first in the Middle East and later in Europe. The manufacture of pottery, followed by the discovery of metals, contributed to the growth of big civilizations and the spreading of urban cultures. These new materials encouraged improvements of existing musical instruments. The materials also led to the invention of new instruments.

"Frozen" Music and Singing Stones

The new agricultural life increased the opportunities for ritualistic ceremonies. The rhythm of the seasons and the sowing and harvesting of crops all called for celebration, as did many of the day-to-day events of a society beginning to put down roots. The role of music inevitably grew in importance and scope; community life demanded songs for work and war.

It was during the Neolithic period, too, that the practice arose of erecting enormous stone monuments; this so-called megalithic culture spread over an area from Southern Asia to Polynesia, on the one hand, and to Western Europe (Spain, Ireland and Scandinavia), on the other. These megaliths are generally reckoned to be some four thousand years old; however, carbon tests on wooden and charcoal remains from a burial mound at Carnac, in Brittany, suggest an age of anything from five thousand to nine thousand years. The significance of these monumental stones, arranged in rows and orientated according to precise astronomical data, remains an enigma. The method used to put such heavy blocks into position (the big Breton *menhir*

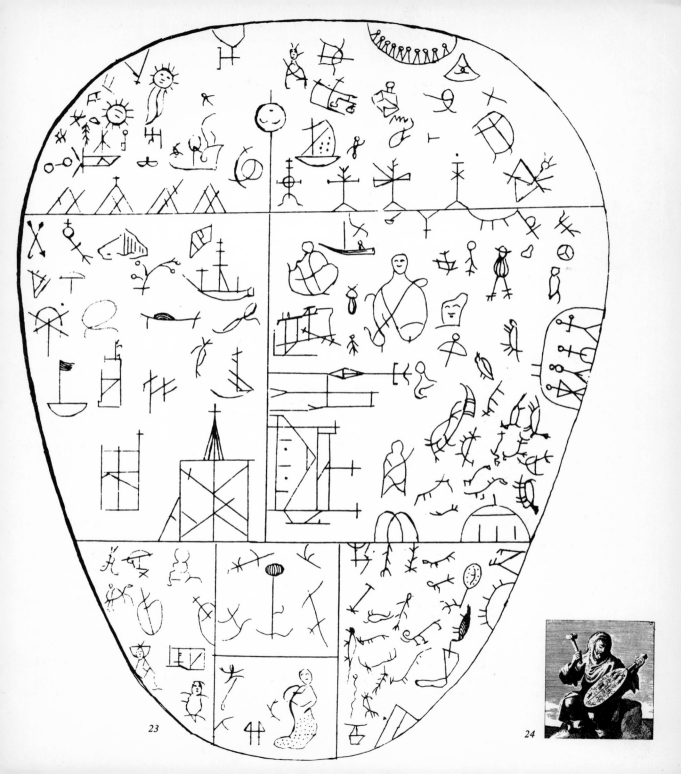

23

24

at Locmariaquer weighs 350 tons) is also a mystery. If we describe them now in some detail, it is because interesting hypotheses have been put forward about them, which are relevant to the history of music.

Assuming that these gigantic edifices were connected with worship—and this seems likely—they may well have been the sites for processions, sacred dances and even combats, of mythological significance. Music must have played a central part in these ceremonies, elaborating them according to their scope. What is more, taking recent research into account,[13] it seems that certain rows of megaliths were actually visible and were concrete symbols of dances or sacred rites. They were a means of consolidating the essential elements of a cult to increase its power. In short, they were "frozen" music. The use of astronomical data to calculate the exact placing of these monuments shows a direct link between the cosmic universe and the world of sound. Perhaps the Ancient Greeks were not the first to believe in the "music of the spheres."

It is not too fanciful to draw a parallel between these megaliths and the "singing stones" (lithophones) of ancient China, or the strange Egyptian statue of Memnon, which gave forth musical sounds with the rays of the rising sun. This was supposed to be the voice of Memnon greeting his mother, Eos (Dawn). The "colossi of Memnon" —a pair of statues near Thebes representing Amenhotep III (*ca.* 1400 B.C.)—were placed at the entrance of his magnificent funerary temple, the rest of which has disappeared.

One final link with the megalithic culture: Marius Schneider believes that there exists today a certain kind of polyphony that dates from Neolithic times. This tradition, discernible in an area stretching from Eastern Europe to the Pacific, embracing the Caucasus, Afghanistan, India, Indonesia and Melanesia, has had such diverse offshoots as the Indonesian orchestra and Western polyphony.

Music of the Nomads: Narrative Song

Despite the tendency toward settled communities, nomadic tribes continued to flourish. Nomads have always had a predilection for the temporal arts, music and poetry, and we are indebted to them for the creation of the narrative song and epic poem. The nomads of Asia to this day have their bards who travel from one encampment to another, reciting to their own accompaniment the legends and heroic deeds of their ancestors.

Musical traditions going back to much earlier

25

times are still kept alive by the herdsmen of Asia and Africa, and the shepherds of the Caucasus and the Alps. At dusk, long-drawn-out melodies based on only three notes are sung wordlessly and with great rhythmic flexibility, to keep the evil spirits away. Generally speaking, the subject matter of their dances and songs—such as the famous "Ranz des Vaches"—concerns the bull or cattle that they revere with an almost religious devotion.[14]

It is interesting that just as the Alpine horn originated in Central Asia, so the art of yodelling is by no means exclusive to the Alps; it is to be met with elsewhere, notably among the African Pygmies. Concerning yodelling and other vocal effects, the following observation by André Schaeffner is relevant: "Primitive man, in creating musical instruments and deforming his voice, wanted to produce sounds that would disguise his human state, just as he camouflaged his body with paint, grass skirts and masks." In other words, we see yet again man's desire to identify himself with the gods.

26

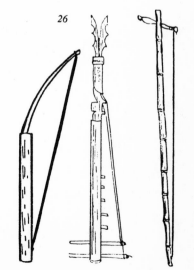

25-26 Various musical bows and rudimentary kitharas.

27 Harpist. (Sumerian stele, tombstone, in terra cotta, height 4 inches—
second half of the 3rd millennium B.C.)

28 Musician. (Sumerian terra cotta fragment—end of the 3rd millennium B.C.)

29 Instrumentalists playing sacred music. (Palace of Tello—Mesopotamia—2400 B.C.)

THE CIVILIZATIONS OF THE NEAR EAST

Mesopotamia
Egypt
Crete
Palestine

The first big urban civilizations arose some five thousand years ago in three distinct areas: between the Tigris and the Euphrates rivers (Mesopotamia), in the Nile Valley (Egypt), and in the Eastern basin of the Mediterranean (Crete).

One of the principal archaeological events of our century has been the discovery of the Sumerian civilization in Lower Mesopotamia. It has revealed the existence of a highly organized society some centuries before the birth of the Egyptian culture. The origin of the Sumerians remains a controversial question, but there is complete agreement about the value of their contributions to civilization. Sumerian society—the first known to have possessed an alphabet, writing, literature, sculpture, architecture (including the first arch, column and vault), a calendar, a rule by law, and a government—must inevitably have had a profound influence on Mesopotamian culture.

Egypt is outstanding for the monumental statuary and Cyclopean architecture she produced. Yet somehow the austere sacredness of these gigantic constructions is always tempered with a touch of humanity. Ancient Egyptian painting and literature show likewise this capacity for expressing the most grandiose ideas in a living art that is at once refined and in touch with reality.

Similarly the Cretans, Hittites, Phoenicians,

30

Syrians and Hebrews developed their own cultures, each with its distinctive features. We know, however, that these societies were in direct contact with each other, and it is not surprising that on such fundamental issues as religion, politics and the arts they shared a view of the world and of man that differed less in principle than in its application.

The role that music played in these civilizations must have been governed by the conventions of everyday life, both sacred and secular. Nevertheless, it is probable that the music of Babylonia, Egypt and Crete showed differences in style as characteristic as those found in the plastic arts and architecture of these diverse peoples.

Beyond this, alas, we cannot judge. True, we have copious pictorial and literary evidence to confirm the central place music occupied in primitive urban societies, but even the discovery of musical instruments in the course of archaeological excavations cannot reconstruct for us the music itself. We must resign ourselves to an imperfect knowledge based on theoretical and historical ideas. The actual sound of this music died with the men and women who played it—all the more tantalizing in view of the many paintings, sculptures and poems of performing musicians still extant. Unless future research proves otherwise, we have to accept the fact that no system of notation has preserved for us a record, say, of Hebrew psalmody, or of the music of Sumeria, the Egyptian Pharaohs, or the luxurious Court of Cnossos; nor is any musical treatise from this period known to exist.

We are reckoning without the oral tradition, however, which in music plays such an important role in keeping the art of one age alive in another. Indeed, there are many respects in which we are still living in the heritage of Sumeria and Egypt. Many of their modes of musical expression are used today, especially in our more primitive societies; some of our musical instruments have not undergone any essential changes for over four thousand years; the foundation of the musical profession itself dates from this time. Food for thought for the modernist at any price! The blind harp player from Sumeria or Egypt, as we see him represented by Mesopotamian sculptors or Egyptian painters, is the spiritual kinsman of the old blind harpist who until only recently played in the busy streets of many sprawling cities. The delicate charm of the girls playing the flute and lute for the Pharaohs, captured in the skillful brush strokes of the fresco painters of Thebes, has never been surpassed; this sensitive figure-drawing, the very embodiment of music in its fluidity of form, is perhaps the most eloquent of all time. The famous

24

30-31 Musicians with angular harps. (fragment of a Sumerian vase— 3300-3000 B.C.)

31

Sumerian text that describes with such engaging informality a day in the life of a schoolboy four thousand years ago could in many respects almost have been written by a youngster today. (The eminent archaeologist, S.N. Kramer, has included this account in his book on Sumeria).[15]

These examples should help to close the gap between early civilizations and our modern world. We need no longer feel at a loss when confronted with the awesome statues of Ur and Babylon; their kinship with medieval sculpture has long been established. Similarly, the religious songs of these peoples have been perpetuated, at least in part, in our own Christian liturgy.

The theocratic states of Sumeria, Babylonia, Assyria and Egypt accorded a fundamental place to religion and the worship of their gods. This, of course, laid great emphasis on the role of music, which was, and still is, intimately bound up with the liturgy.

Song Enhances the Power of Speech

Despite superficial resemblances, however, it is on the spiritual level that primitive societies differ radically from our own. Whereas our ideology is based on rationalism, theirs was inherently religious. This, of course, conditioned the place of music in their lives. For us it has become an entertainment giving aesthetic pleasure, but for them it was essentially a means of communication with the supernatural, of allaying evil spirits, or of achieving a state of trance.

In Sumeria, music was given such pride of place that it was included in the list of divine laws and fundamentals of civilization. "A good thousand years before the Hebrews wrote their Bible, and the Greeks their Iliad and Odyssey, there already existed a flourishing literary tradition in the form of myths and epic poems, hymns and lamentations, and numerous collections of proverbs, fables and essays."[16] Musical instruments were placed in the same category as divine beings, cosmic forces, and other essentials in the smooth running of human society.

All over the world, since time immemorial, the liturgy has been sung. The power of music increases the effectiveness of speech, exalting it, and making it worthy of the Throne of God. Even a spell has more potency if the magic words are sung. Witness the serenade, which was originally a form of amatory enchantment. Not long ago, itinerant preachers in Europe and the East used to sing their sermons, emulating the old prophets. Still today the Jews follow a tradition that no doubt goes back to the Levites, in that public read-

25

32

ings from the Bible are set to different melodies for each Book.

The Birth of Liturgical Music

In Sumeria as in Egypt, music (performed by instrumental and choral ensembles) belonged to the activities of the Temple, which was the hub of the spiritual and intellectual life of the city; even the schools and libraries depended on it. The priest-musicians, a rich and powerful class, developed a liturgy based on the mythological life of the gods, the important episodes of which were celebrated with processions, ceremonies and great religious feasts.

The hymns and prayers were performed with an instrumental accompaniment of strings, wind or percussion, the choice of instruments depending on the god being worshiped and the nature of the ceremony. Likewise, according to the liturgical feast, songs of praise and jubilation or of lamentation and penitence were sung.

Although there are no existing musical examples, here at least are the fragments of two hymns. The first was composed to celebrate the building of a temple to the Sumerian god, Enki E'engourra. The term *algars* mentioned in the first line refers to a type of lyre:

Lyres, algars, harps, drums,
Sistra, instruments of Sabum and Maeri which fill
the house,
The sweet voice of harps,
Let them resound before his terrible magnificence!
Let the terrible and magnificent instrument of
Enki, the sacred algar, sound forth,
Let all musicians play!

The second is dedicated to Hathor, the Egyptian goddess of love and music:

"We jubilate before thy presence, oh sovereign of Denderah . . . thou art the queen of jubilation, the sovereign of those who sing, the queen of those who dance, the sovereign of those who weave garlands. Come, shout for joy, and bang the drum day and night! The men bang the drum and the women rejoice. . . ."[17]

Sumeria established the foundations of a liturgical tradition inseparably linked with music, the form of which was to have a powerful influence on subsequent civilizations. We owe to the Sumerians the structure of the psalm, for instance, where each verse falls into two parallel sections expressing the same thought in different ways. The verses alternated with refrains, and Walter Wiora believes that the verses were sung by a cantor and

26

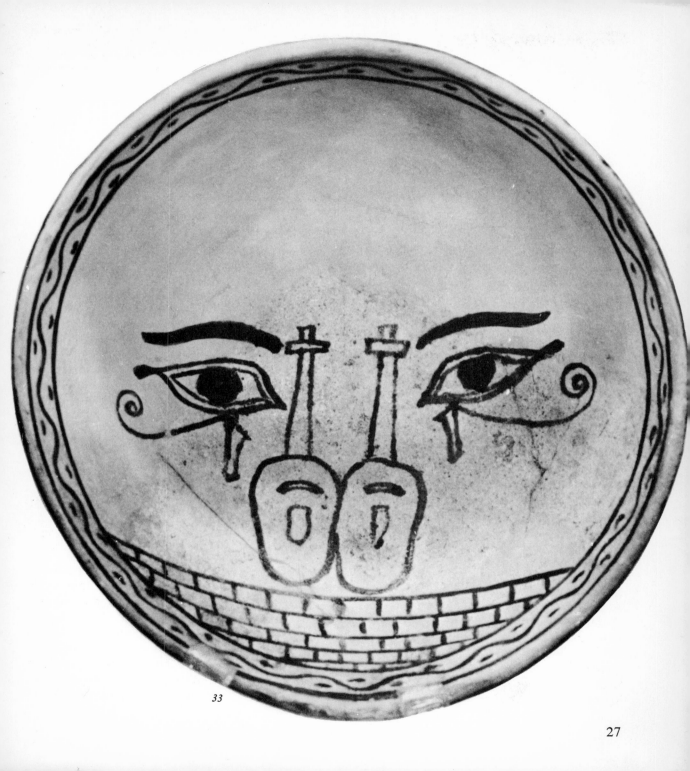

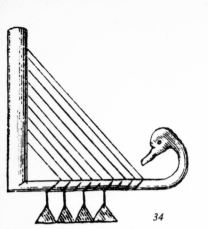

35

34

the refrains by the congregation, as in the ancient Jewish service, and later in the responsorial psalmody of the Christian Church. What is certain, as the musicologist A. Machabey has observed, is that Sumerian litany became integrated "with the cult of Mithra (god of day) in Persia and that of Cybele (mother of the gods) in Asia Minor, then proceeded to Rome, where the Christian litany, itself of Syrian origin, joined it and ultimately spread throughout the West."[18]

"The extraordinary spiritual permanence of the Sumerians during the whole history of Babylonia and Assyria is explained in that up to a hundred years before the Christian era the Mesopotamian Semites retained the Sumerian languages for scientific and liturgical purposes, much as Western kingdoms still used Latin in the Middle Ages."[18]

Processions

As the general public was not permitted to worship in the sanctuary of the temple, open-air religious ceremonies gave rise to imposing processions and great celebrations, especially in Egypt. The men played their flutes, and the women their krotala (similar to castanets). When the Pharaoh and his court took part in these spectacles, they were transformed into full-scale national festivals.

Let us picture the annual festival of Min, the god of fecundity in Egypt in the Middle Kingdom period. The Pharaoh, carried on a sumptuous litter by royal princes and state officials, and followed by a retinue of dignitaries, is making his way to the temple. As he arrives, the doors are solemnly opened, and a hymn is sung, with dancing. The sacred statue is withdrawn from its naos (inner chamber) and hoisted on to another litter, borne by twenty-two priests. The Pharaoh now heads the procession, accompanied by his queen, and also by a white bull, the incarnation of Min; a sun-like disc, surmounted by two plumes, gleams between its horns. The procession slowly advances to a specially constructed shrine, with hymn-singing and dancing at every halt. When the shrine is reached, the Pharaoh changes his headdress and regalia several times, in symbolical homage to the creative and fecund powers of the god.[19]

Often these festivals were elaborated with dramatic representations, which usually evoked the outstanding episodes in the life of a god. According to Breasted, the Egyptologist, these performances were not unlike the mystery plays of our Middle Ages. The priests of Babylon, during processional rites for their god Marduk, also presented sacred dramas, depicting his death and resurrection.[20]

28

34 *Egyptian angular harp.*
35 *Egyptian arched harp.*
36 *Sistrum. (dating from Roman times)*

36

Although no written evidence has survived, we are justified in assuming that music must have played a prominent part in these dramatic representations.

Rites and Sacred Dances

A few words about the hymns accompanied by the dancing. The dance has always been the handmaiden of music, whether secular or sacred. Religious rites were danced as well as sung, even on solemn occasions, such as a funeral ceremony. When David danced in front of the Ark, he worshiped his God no less sincerely than the Pharaoh who danced before the statue of his deity in the Holy of Holies of the Temple. Just as song elevates speech from its functional level to a higher plane, so the dance transcends the stereotyped gestures of our everyday life. As the French poet, Paul Valéry, once said of a dancer: "She has only to walk, and behold, she is a goddess; and we feel like gods. . . ."

Music, a Way of Provoking Ecstasy

Music and dance were also used as a means of provoking a state of trance, ecstasy, mystical delirium, or spiritual inspiration—in short, of inducing divine "possession." We find numerous examples of this in the Bible.[21] The chronicler tells us that the prophet Saul, having listened to the music of the lyre, drum, flute and harp, had a vision, and the Spirit of the Lord came upon him. (I Samuel 10 and I Samuel 19).

Man's thirst for the mystical is unquenchable. Consider the visions of the prophets of Israel; the exaltation of the worshipers of Dionysus, the god of wine; the excitement bordering on hysteria of the followers of Astarte, the Syrian nature goddess, at Damascus (flutes and drums played their part here); and the ecstasy, even today, of the dancing dervishes of Islam or of the Siberian shamans.

Music and Magic

In another story about Saul, we find an example of the healing powers of music in the soul's struggle against possession by the devil. (In an age when mental disorders were attributed to the influence of evil spirits, the therapeutic value of music and magic can hardly be overestimated.) When Saul suffered an attack of melancholia, he placed himself in the care of his harpist: "David took his harp and played; then Saul was calmed and the evil spirit departed from him." (I Samuel 16).

The inanimate world was not completely immune to the omnipotence of sound; indeed, it was

29

the combined powers of magic and music that made the walls of Jericho crumble. After a sevenfold procession round the city, which accumulated a terrible destructive force at the center of the magic circle, Joshua ordered the fatal sounding of the trumpets.

If we are still sceptical, let us refer again to Paul Valéry, who is not generally associated with mysticism: "Music—ecstatic, demoniac, visionary, soul-consuming—offers us, indeed imposes on us, a dreamworld that is more potent than the world we live in."

Crete

Unfortunately, the religious life of the Cretans is scantily documented. It seems that these people did not possess temples, but erected their shrines quite indiscriminately in such incongruous settings as palace courtyards, grottoes, and mountain tops.[22]

The few paintings and illuminations on which we rely, however, suggest that ritualistic worship was by no means unfamiliar to the Cretans. When we see pictures of priests and priestesses dancing round a sacred tree or a statue of a god, and elsewhere a flautist playing his instrument behind a sacred bull destined for sacrifice, we can only conclude that these performers were taking part in sacred rites.

Music at Court, Secular Music

Just as the priest-musicians represented the religious hierarchy, so the minstrels and bards were associated with royalty. From the time of the ancient Sumerian civilization onward, we find constant references to the relationship between music and epic literature. Furthermore, as S. N. Kramer has pointed out, there are striking resemblances between the religious, social and artistic doctrines of successive ages; he cites the "heroic ages" of Sumeria (first quarter of the 3rd millennium B.C.), Greece (end of the 2nd millennium B.C.), India (about a hundred years later), and the Germanic peoples (4th to 6th centuries A.D.). Each of these civilizations created legends in the form of epic poetry, which must have been recited or, more probably, sung. "The governing classes craved above all for glory. The bards were therefore commissioned to improvise narrative poems in which they had to extol the brave exploits of their kings and princes. These tales served to entertain the guests at the feasts and banquets given by the rulers, and were probably recited with the accompaniment of a lyre or harp."[23] Nine of these Sumerian epic poems have been recovered to date; they vary in length between about a hundred and just over six hundred lines.

30

37 *Funeral banquet.*
Bas-relief decorating a tomb.
(Ancient Empire period)
38 *Banqueting scene.*
(Thebes—1500 B.C.)

38

The task of music, then, was to reflect the magnificence and power of royalty. Besides the bards, the kings and Pharaohs maintained harems of singers, dancers and instrumentalists, and also temple choirs, whose fame often spread throughout the whole kingdom. During the sumptuous feasts and ritual banquets held at court, these performers soothed the ears of the guests with their music. It is significant that after expeditions of war, the vanquished had to give up not only their women and riches, but also their choirs and orchestras. A bas-relief mural from Nineveh (in the British Museum) depicts just such a surrender. The group of musicians handed over consists of eleven performers, "who do not seem to have been chosen at random; their arrangement shows a sure knowledge of the blend of instruments and tone-colors" (Claude Frissard).[24] They are followed by a chorus of nine children and six women.

From this period onward we see the aristocracy and upper-class people drawing their inspiration from the behavior fashionable at court or in the big city centers, and then cultivating these customs and extravagances themselves. This is certainly true of music, especially in Egypt, where the art seems to have been pursued avidly by all classes of society. (The numerous illustrations of musicians in Egyptian frescoes bear this out.) Even agricul-

tral work was carried out to music; harvesting, fruit-picking and grape-gathering were all accompanied by singing and the playing of instruments. At mealtimes in well-to-do households, when the maids brought in the food, musicians entered, too, singing and playing their sistra and krotalas. Sometimes an acrobat would mingle with the performers, who improvised verses in honor of the guests or of the gods.

Wealthy Egyptians, who delighted in surrounding themselves with beautiful ornaments and precious works of art, spent many of their leisure hours listening to the music of the flute and the lyre. Their womenfolk, on the other hand, preferred the harp, the kithara, the lute or the drum. The same was true of the rich people of Babylonia and Assyria. (We know, furthermore, that the customs of Babylonia were copied in all the big cities of the Eastern Mediterranean.)

In Mesopotamia the ordinary citizens seem to have been no less addicted to music than the aristocracy. They looked upon any feast-day as an excuse for merrymaking and music; in a Sumerian text describing a festival in honor of Ishtar, we read, "The people of Kichi are dancing, rattling their sistra in their left hands; the city center re-echoes to the sound of cymbals, and from further away comes the music of panpipes and drums."

31

39

40

Sometimes music served an unusual purpose. When the Assyrian king Ashurbanipal wanted to rebuild his palace, he forced the kings of Arabia, whom he had vanquished, "to carry laborers' kit-bags and to wear workmen's caps." "They spent their days molding bricks and undergoing forced labor, to the sound of music. Thus I completed my building cheerfully and briskly. . . ."[25]

Incidentally, we must not imagine that this music was designed merely to entertain the workmen; it was a way of ensuring that the work was accomplished harmoniously, and to the satisfaction of the gods.

We return now to the Cretans, whose civilization was undoubtedly one of the most advanced in the ancient world, with an artistic tradition that shows an unparalleled refinement. Surely the acute sensitivity of these people must have been reflected in their music! At Cnossos and Phaestos the earliest known theatres have been discovered, dating from about 2000 B.C., and with a seating capacity of four or five hundred. What kind of performances were given there? Dramas? Dancing, accompanied by singers and instrumentalists? Of one thing we can be certain: music must have contributed to the spectacles intended for those pleasure-seeking people of ancient Crete.

The Musicians: Their Status and Duties

In societies so alive with music, it was inevitable that the musical profession should develop quickly along independent lines. Even the harpists and singers depicted on Sumerian statuary belonged to authorized organizations, although we do not know whether membership was by birth or by subscription.

The rank of a musician depended on his function. If he was attached to the temple he formed part of the hierarchy of priests; his prestige was considerable, especially if he was the cantor for an important god. He took the lead in processions, his priestly status automatically placing him next in line below the gods and the king, and therefore above the scribes. If he directed a choir-school, his position was equivalent to that of the overlord of the palace or of the chief eunuch.

Many female singers and dancers were associated with the temple as concubines of the god. Their domain was the sanctuary devoted to goddesses, where they formed a school of sacred courtesans. (It seems that such an establishment was incorporated in the temple of the Egyptian goddess, Hathor, sister of the Greek Aphrodite and the Babylonian Ishtar.) It might be thought that an affiliation of this sort would have been shameful

33

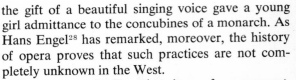

41

42

for young girls, but in fact the opposite was true. Our Western morality, with all its hypocrisy, has made us draw a veil over these institutions, especially as we do not really understand their true significance.

According to J. Evola,[26] the Italian scholar who has thrown some light on the subject, the courtesans, or handmaids of the goddess, solemnized the mysteries of carnal love by actively taking part in a magic rite. In doing so they maintained a psychic link, symbolized in bodily unity, with their goddess, and also transmitted the virtue of the goddess to those who joined with them in the performance of the sacrament. The maidens were variously called "pure," "virginal" and "saintly." In principle, this union has the same function as the sacrament of the Eucharist: it represents man's communion with the *sacrum,* held and administered by the woman.

In India and Syria,[27] the temple dancers were also employed as courtesans of the gods. Evola tells us that even the highest families considered it an honor for their daughters to be chosen from infancy to be consecrated to the service of the temple.

If we dwell at some length on this intimacy between music and Eros, it is because the musical profession has been linked with the courtesan since remotest antiquity. In certain Oriental societies,

the gift of a beautiful singing voice gave a young girl admittance to the concubines of a monarch. As Hans Engel[28] has remarked, moreover, the history of opera proves that such practices are not completely unknown in the West.

To return to the Egyptian singers for a moment, we find that those who served in the *khenerit* (the most sacred part of a sanctuary or palace) had to reside at the temple. Their leader was known as the god's divine concubine, handmaid or worshiper. The true wife of the god was the queen herself, whose duty it was to conduct the choir of courtesans.[29] Many musicians were also employed at court, some of whom held posts of considerable prestige value. We actually know the names of certain Sumerian and Egyptian court musicians: in Egypt the master of royal music some time between 2723 B.C. and 2563 B.C. was Hemrē; the inspector of song about 2423 B.C. was Snefrounofer I, who in his dual capacity as Chancellor of the Exchequer had to present himself daily to the Pharaoh.[30] The royal concubines looked after the teams of dancers and supervised on state occasions.

It seems that musicians then, as today, practiced their art with varying degrees of success, according to their talent and position; they were either highly respected or treated with disdain. For instance, we read of Egyptian harpists being suspended from

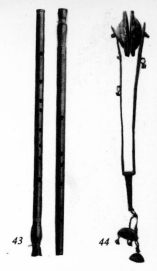

41 Wooden krotala (castanets) in the shape of a hand. These instruments were probably used in the worship of Hathor, the goddess of music and love.
42 Metal sistrum (Late Empire period—ca. 500 B.C.)
43 Wooden flutes.
44 Cymbals. (dating from the Roman period)

43   44

their services at royal banquets for being gluttonous and dirty.[31] An interesting point is that Egyptian harpists had their heads shaved as a sign of consecration; also, many of them were blind. (There are records of blind harpists, too, in Japan and Ireland, and among certain Negro chieftains. Could this affliction originally have had some mystical or symbolical significance? We cannot be sure, Even today there is an aura of mystique surrounding our blind organists.)

If we examine the graceful forms of the female musicians delineated by Egyptian fresco painters, we cannot help being struck by another odd feature: whereas the harpists and flautists are clothed, the lutenists are nearly always naked, as we know the servants and slaves to have been in all strata of society. Must we conclude from this that the lute was not considered to be such a noble instrument as the harp, lyre or flute, or simply that it served a different purpose? Suffice it to say that this strange anomaly of dress appears frequently in Egyptian frescoes.

In short, then, we see musicians contributing to the life of the community on every level: from the dignitaries of the court or temple to the village singers and instrumentalists, not forgetting the wandering minstrels, who roamed the countryside with warriors and merchants, or quite alone. The musical profession in those far-off times was indeed varied—almost as varied as it is today.

Instruments

It is now known that most of the musical instruments inherited by our European civilization from the Mediterranean peoples originally came from ancient Mesopotamia.[32]

In Sumeria the harp was a royal instrument, as it was in Egypt.[33] Two types of Sumerian harp existed: the vertical and the horizontal. The vertical kind was not unlike our own in appearance, but for the absence of a fore-pillar; it was held against the player's chest, and the strings were plucked directly by the fingers. The horizontal harp, however, was played with a plectrum, and here again the framework did not completely enclose the instrument. In the British Museum is the eleven-stringed harp of Queen Shub-ad; its animal's head is encrusted with precious metals and lapis-lazuli.

As A. Schaeffner has pointed out, the lyres and kitharas (strung horizontally and diagonally) discovered in the royal tombs at Ur prove that already some five thousand years ago there was a high standard of stringed instrument-making. The extravagant ornamentation on these instruments indicates their royal or religious function.[34]

35

45 *Cretan dancers in terra cotta. (Palaikastro, Crete)*

The Sumerian long-necked lute dates from about 2000 B.C. It had two or three strings, plucked with a plectrum, and a small body in the shape of a half-pear.

Mesopotamian wind instruments included the flute, end-blown like the recorder; the aulos, a twin-piped, double-reeded instrument, ancestor of the oboe; and the trumpet. A silver aulos from a tomb at Ur is in the University Museum at Philadelphia.

Of the percussion instruments, the largest was the *balag,* which seems to have been a gigantic bass drum, or perhaps even a gong. (Sumerian musical terminology is exceptionally obscure.) The instrument was surmounted by a figurine of a ram's head, representing Ea, the goddess of exorcism, to whom the balag was dedicated. According to contemporary documents, the hollow sound it made resembled the muffled bellowing of a wild bull. There were also smaller drums, conical or cylindrical in shape, and oblong or circular tambourines. Other popular percussion instruments were the bronze cymbals and kettledrums, and the rattle-like sistrum.

In Egypt, we find that the instruments in use from the time of the Pyramids were the flute, the double clarinet (two single-reeded pipes paired together) and, of course, the harp. They were played alone, in duets or trios, or to accompany voices.

With the advent of the New Empire, the variety within each family of instruments grew enormously. The harp, for instance, could be small and portable, larger and fixed on a stand, or truly monumental, with more strings and a proportionately wider compass. This latter type was richly decorated with floral and geometrical designs, the frame extending to form a carved head of gilded wood. Apparently, Egyptian harpists used their fingers rather than a plectrum to pluck the strings.

The lyre and kithara showed a similar diversity of forms. The kithara varied from an elegant portable type, with only five strings, to a man-sized model played by two musicians standing up. The Egyptian lute had four strings but was otherwise similar to its Sumerian predecessor, with its small body and long neck.

The flute, too, increased in size and melodic range. The aulos at this time was made of two pipes forming an acute angle, and the double clarinet of parallel pipes.

The drum was less popular in Egypt than it had been in Sumeria, but the tambourine was retained in both its round and oblong forms. The krotala, like the sistrum, was dedicated to the goddess

37

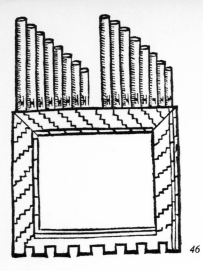

46

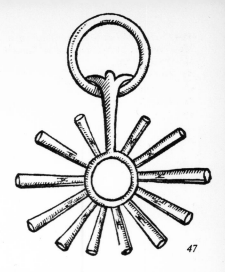

47

Hathor. It was equivalent to our castanets, being made of two clappers of wood or ivory on a chain. The sistrum was composed of small metal discs.

Finally, we must mention an instrument whose origins remain obscure—the organ. It seems that a *hydraulis* (water organ) was invented during the 3rd century B.C. by an Egyptian, Ktesibios of Alexandria. Its name derives from the skillfully devised hydraulic mechanism that fed the pipes with air. The instrument was also used in Rome to accompany gladiatorial shows.

In Crete, we find evidence of an instrument the Greeks claimed was invented by Terpander, born some thousand years later! This is the seven-stringed lyre, depicted on a sarcophagus of the Cretan, Hagia Triada. Also shown here is a double flute with eight holes. On a Cretan cameo we see a woman playing a trumpet made of an enormous conch. Like their Egyptian sisters, the Cretans accompanied themselves with the sistrum.

Instrumental Ensembles

How were the instruments tuned? Was a pentatonic or heptatonic system used? Musicologists have put forward various theories, which, though undoubt-edly interesting, are still in the realms of specula-tion.[35]

It has been proved, however, that as far back as the Sumerian era, musicians delighted in mingling the tone-colors of voices and instruments (kitharas, flutes, harps, sistra, drums, trumpets). In Assyria these ensembles played an important part in cere-monial life; during the reign of King Solomon, no less than 120 trumpeters performed at the con-secration of the temple.

Musicians in these early civilizations seem to have had a fine ear for instrumental coloring. It is doubtless going too far to suggest that they prac-ticed true polyphony, but they must have exploited all the resources of heterophony (modified versions of the same melody by various performers, perhaps with the accompaniment of a drone). If we con-sider that primitive races today, with no cultural background whatever, use heterophony verging on polyphony, we may reasonably assume that the great civilizations of the past—with their stagger-ing achievements of creative imagination in archi-tecture, sculpture, painting and literature, as well as in the various crafts—would have been dissatis-fied with a random juxtaposition of notes or tone-colors in their music.

46-49 *Hebrew instruments. (illustrations taken from*
Musurgia, seu praxis, musicae *by Luscinius,*
Strasbourg, 1536)
46 *Organ.*
47 *Cymbals.*
48 *Trumpet.*
49 *Type of gong.*

48

Egyptian Cheironomy

Musical cheironomy is a system of hand signs designed to remind the performers of the direction of a melody, and to indicate inflections of rhythm. Its practice goes back to remotest antiquity, but it was the Egyptians in particular who over a period of centuries carried the art to an extraordinary level of refinement.

The "cheironomist" or "metronomist" was, in effect, the conductor of the instrumental or vocal group in his charge. Indeed, his role was even more vital than that of our modern conductor; the performers had no written music in front of them—it seems that music-making was exclusively an oral tradition at this time—and so relied on him entirely to remind them of the tune. It must not be thought that these indications were merely a series of vague gestures; on the contrary, they formed a detailed and precise system of arm, hand and finger movements, which the players or singers interpreted accordingly. The German musicologist, Hans Hickmann, has attempted to decipher this system, with convincing results.[36]

49

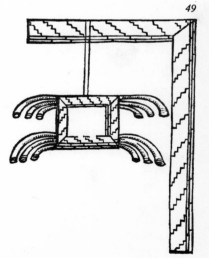

The archaeological excavations carried out in the 1920's at Mohenjo-Daro, on the banks of the Lower Indus River, revealed an urban civilization dating from the 4th millennium B.C. This seems to have been strikingly similar to the contemporary Sumerian culture; indeed, the existence of bathrooms, plumbing systems, cooking utensils, and superbly wrought jewelry in gold and silver, suggests an even higher level of achievement than that of the Sumerians. One cannot help wondering how such an advanced civilization, with its own sculpture, painting, dance forms and music, came into being. The riddle remains unsolved.

As a background to understand Indian music, here is a brief outline of the history of India.

Brief Historical Survey

About 1500 B.C.: Between 1500 B.C. and 1200 B.C., the Aryans invaded India and superimposed on Hinduism their own Vedic culture (named after the Vedas, the four books of sacred writings including traditional knowledge and also a collection of hymns and chants).

6th century B.C.: Beginning of the Buddhistic period, which lasted about a thousand years.

9th century A.D.: Under the influence of Shankara, at this time, Hinduism regained lost ground,

51 *Mongolian dancer.*

completely supplanting the teachings of Buddha; it managed to retain its identity even after the Muslim conquest.

10th century A.D.: The beginning of the Muslim conquest.

1690: The founding of Calcutta by the English.

Mythological Sources of Indian Music

Despite certain similarities between the musical conceptions of the Indians and the Ancient Greeks, Indian musicians did not share the Greeks' fascination with mathematical speculation.

The origins of Indian music are closely related to mythology, and this link has remained strong until comparatively recently. It is impossible to gain more than a superficial, and indeed uncharacteristic, view of Indian music without taking into account the background of religious beliefs and metaphysical doctrines.

Remember, too, that in India, as in all Oriental countries, music is inseparable from dancing, poetry and mime.

According to ancient Indian beliefs, music stems directly from the supreme godhead and from his chief representatives. For instance, Brahma sang the traditional Vedas, reiterating them incessantly. Rudra, the god of lightning and associated with

song and dance, played the *vina* (stick zither, still popular in India today). The "Eternal Law" of the universe was symbolized in a cosmic dance in which the god played the drum (*damaru*), an instrument revered as the primary source of all sound. From the flute of Mahavishnu sprang melodies of life and evolution; to his music the *Gopis* (incarnations of cosmic forces) sang and danced in celestial harmony, their hands and feet rippling like waves.[37] Just as our heavens resound to the singing of seraphim and cherubim, archangels and all the angels of the celestial hierarchy, so in India the firmaments are filled with music of the celestial bards (*Gandharvas*) and dancers (*Apsaras*).

Man was by no means excluded from this concert. His whole body absorbed the exuberant sounds bestowed on him by the gods. Music affected his stomach, his heart and his head. "To his stomach, where organic reflexes occur, music accords changes of texture, tone-color and intensity. To his heart, where feelings of pleasure and sorrow, desire and aversion originate, it dedicates melody. To his head, fount of intelligence, it devotes rhythm, the very essence of life."[38]

It is evident that in such a context music could never be simply a means of entertainment. To sing or play an instrument is to serve the gods, indeed to unify oneself with them. In a way the gods,

42

52 Indian musicians.

being born of primordial sound, actually personify music. Even St. John said: "In the beginning was the word."

Just as sound created the gods and imposed its rhythm on the universe, so music, which is organized and rhythmic sound, inevitably had a powerful effect on the supernatural, and indeed on the very heavens themselves. So as to uphold the order of the world, great stress was laid on the correct intonation of hymns and ritual formulas. These principles of performance, still adhered to today—despite intervening Buddhist and Islamic influences—were first set out in the *Rigveda* (Veda of Hymns) and the *Samaveda* (Veda of Chants), two of the four sacred Veda books (1500 B.C. to 500 B.C.). According to the oldest Hindu treatises,[39] the seven notes of the Vedic scale correspond to the seven stages in the descent of the divine word into the realms of substance.

It has often been pointed out that there is a similarity between the scale-forms of India and the modes of the European Middle Ages, explained by a common Aryan heritage. W. Wiora has drawn attention to the kinship between certain melodic formulas of the Rigveda and Samaveda and those of Ambrosian and Gregorian chant; both are based on the tetrachord (range of four notes),[40] despite the theoretical seven-note scale mentioned above.

This affinity cannot be extended to the rhythmic element, however. A. A. Bake[41] has observed in this connection that whereas melody is attributed to Brahma, an Aryan god, rhythm is ascribed to Shiva, a non-Aryan god.

The System of Ragas

The raga is essentially a Hindu creation, dominating the musical scene in India from about A.D. 500 to the present day. It is difficult to give a comprehensive definition of the raga. It has an infinite variety of forms, and furthermore, the term implies not only a precise combination of notes and intervals, but also the emotion aroused by them. The actual choice of sounds is only a starting point, moreover. It is the method of putting them together and of placing certain intervals in relief that creates the desired emotional atmosphere, and gives each raga its individual character and hypnotic power. Another variant in the raga is a scale formation that is different ascending from descending.

In Indian musical theory, the octave is divided into sixty-six intervals, called *srutis*.[42]

In practice, however, there are only twenty-two srutis (approximately equivalent to quarter-tones), which are the material from which the two basic seven-note scales are formed. Each of the

43

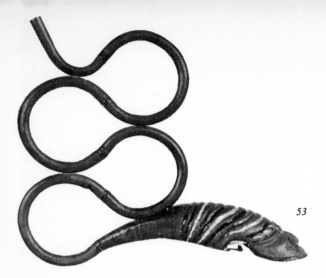

53

seven notes represents a part of the body, namely the soul, the head, the arms, the breast, the neck, the hips and the feet. These notes are also associated with the nerve centers of the human body.[43] The musician has, then, twenty-two srutis from which to choose in forming a raga. By no means any combination of intervals will create a satisfactory melodic formula, however. In theory it seems possible to compose unlimited new ragas, yet in practice only a few hundred are in current use.

Originally, there were only six basic ragas, cited by the sage Bharata in his treatise "Natya Sastra." These corresponded to the six Indian seasons: summer, the monsoons, autumn, early winter, winter and spring. Later theorists added thirty *raginis* (the feminine version), which brought the total of primary ragas to seventy-two, bearing in mind that each one had two scale-forms. At the height of the classical period, the number of ragas ran into thousands, but it is doubtful whether more than a small proportion of these were actually used.

Indian music differs fundamentally from its European counterpart in that it is always improvised. Two ragas using the identical combination of intervals would vary considerably in detail, despite their common overall structure. In the north of India, the following raga pattern is usual: the first section presents the theme, which is followed by three improvised variations, each in a different register (within a range of three octaves). In the chant form, the unadorned melody is repeated after each variation.

According to Indian theory, each raga has a specific aesthetic and social function. It is linked with a certain season or lunar period, with a precise hour of day or night, and with a specific place, whether palace or pasture. Failure to observe these conventions leads to unrest in the heavens and in the human soul, just as false intonation has catastrophic results in the realms of the spirits and angels. There are some ragas (called *dipakas*) that cause a ring of fire to encircle any musician foolhardy enough to use them; others attract serpents; still others bring rain, especially if they are played by a young girl.[44] Put another way, it is as unthinkable for an orthodox Hindu musician to play a raga unsuitable for the occasion as for a Western organist to perform a funeral march at a wedding.[45]

What especially strikes the Westerner on hearing a raga is its uniformity (which is not to suggest monotony). Whereas our musical ideal is that of a variety of moods within a balanced whole, the Indian raga, like Iranian or Arabic music, is concerned with exhausting all the possibilities of a single emotion.

In northern India, the raga system has been

53 Indian trumpet.
54 Sesando, the national instrument of
the Isle of Roti in Indonesia.
It is a sort of bamboo kithara,
with 10 to 36 copper strings, and a
sound box made from a palm leaf.
55 Detail of a trumpet
made of bronze and leather.

54

55

45

56 *Vina, a typically Indian stringed instrument, dedicated to Sarasvati, the goddess of wisdom. The player rests one of the gourd sound boxes on his left shoulder, stopping the strings with his left hand and plucking them with his right, sometimes with the aid of a plectrum.*

56

carried to a high degree of emotional refinement. From the time of the Muslim conquest (from about A.D. 1000), a gradual divergence of styles occurred between the music of northern and southern India. While the south remained relatively immune to the Muslim influence, the north assimilated it and gradually created a form of music that was at once powerful and elegant—"neither Muslim nor Hindu, but Indian in the true sense of the word," as one modern Indian writer has put it.[46] In southern India, music evolved on different lines; it remained more austere, and in fact closer to the old Hindu culture and that of the popular religions of Shiva and Vishnu.

Music and the Senses

The Hindus established a precise relationship between music, poetry and *rasa* (literally 'savor,' but more broadly "perception"). "The concept of rasa is central to Hindu aesthetics," asserts René Daumal. We find the idea again, though in a slightly different form, in the Far East. "Rasa, in establishing an emotional contact between the individual and the laws of the universe, is essentially a cognition. It is the conscious joy felt even in response to the artistic portrayal of sorrowful subjects, which, being mere shadows of the realities of everyday

life, are elevated to a higher plane."[47] (This definition could equally well be applied to a Beethoven Adagio, where sorrow seems to be sublimated by art.)

The Hindu angels and *Gandharvas* (celestial musicians), on the other hand, associated music with scents, "for ideas and emotions are carried along by the stream of music like a perfume on the breeze, without the intervention of analysis" (Alain Daniélon).[48]

These ideas, alien though they are to our Western philosophy, are well worth considering in our attempt to delve more deeply into the musical concepts of the Orient. They bear witness to the subtlety with which Hindu writers have analyzed the psychological effects of art.

Rhythm and Instruments

The rhythm of Indian music is extremely complex. It is based on the *tala,* a fixed rhythmic pattern, often very long and subdivided into four sections, which is reiterated throughout a piece of music. The players are then free to decorate this basic pattern with further rhythmic intricacies. The interplay between the talas of different instruments produces polyrhythms every bit as subtle as our Western polyphony. Attempts to codify and classify the ragas have shown that in theory at least they number 120, each bearing a different name.

It is hardly surprising that percussion or "rhythm" instruments are particularly important in India. The drum, for instance, appears in many forms; it can be made of terra cotta, wood or metal, and can be played with drumsticks, the palm of the hand, or the fingers. Cymbals are also popular for rhythmic accompaniments.

Stringed instruments come in two categories, depending on whether the strings are plucked or bowed. In the first group are the *vina,* the *sitar* and the *sarod,* all types of zither, and in the second the *sarangi,* the *esraj* and the *dilruha.* The *tamboura* (a four-stringed lute) is used only as a drone accompaniment.

Wind instruments are represented by vertical and transverse bamboo flutes; by two varieties of oboe, the *shannai* and *nagaswaram,* one played in the north and the other in the south, but both of Islamic origin; by the conch, reserved for use in the temple; and by the trumpet, which is often over two yards long.

Today, the violin and clarinet are familiar in India, and also, alas, "the abominable portative harmonium," introduced by the missionaries.[49] (The harmonium itself was partly an adaptation of the Chinese *sheng,* imported into Europe around 1800.)

Music in Indian Life

With a people so naturally gifted in poetry and mysticism, it is not surprising that for a long time vocal music prevailed over instrumental music. (Vedic chant dates from as early as 1000 B.C.)[50] Hindu mythology does mention some use of instruments, however, especially as an accompaniment for dancing. This custom was reflected in everyday life; the divine flute of Krishna doubtless had its earthly counterparts. The main musical centers were the temples and royal courts. It was the responsibility of the temple musicians to train the choristers and to organize sacred representations, where ritual dances, music and hymns were combined to portray the divine epics.

As in Mesopotamia, the temple maintained troupes of female dancers and singers, called "servants of the gods." "They are richly clad, divinely beautiful, and graceful in their movements," we learn from the Rigveda, the oldest of the four books of Vedas. Some of these musicians, who, incidentally, had a better general education than most girls, appeared at both public and private functions. In short, they played a similar role to that of the Japanese geishas and to that of the Greek courtesans.[51]

Later, the monasteries served to uphold the

57

58

48

57 Man playing the ravanatta,
a popular instrument similar
to the violin.
58 A drum player.
59 A performer on the sarangi,
a bowed instrument.
60-62 Hindu musicians, playing
drums and a gong.

60

61

62

49

63

64

traditions of vocal and instrumental music. Some monasteries maintained their own resident orchestras, which would play at annual festivals and religious ceremonies, while others imported musicians from outside on these occasions.

Music at court was originally strictly functional. The *Raghu Vamca* tells us that one of the court nobleman's duties was to lull the king to sleep and awaken him with music-making. He also had to "mark the passing hours with the correct sequence of melodic modes" (H. Sauvageot). According to the Atharva-Veda, the master of the king's music (*purohita*) had to be conversant with the spiritual qualities of different kinds of music, and to choose a suitable type for each occasion. He was, of course, indispensable on the battlefield, where he would chant musical formulas fitting for each army, and sing hymns to give the warrior power.[52]

Gradually music was secularized, however, and the magic aspect gave way to aesthetic considerations. Princes maintained orchestras for entertainment rather than for ritualistic purposes, and poet musicians were employed to sing the traditional epics. Some of the rulers of India were themselves among the greatest bards in the country (Krishna Raya in the 16th century, for example), and many noblemen of the 17th and 18th centuries distinguished themselves by their musical ability. Even today song, music and dance form an integral part of the education of the upper classes in India.

Every royal residence included a ballroom, and the dancers were generally held in great esteem by their princely patrons. A passage from the great epic *Mahabharata* (400 B.C.–A.D. 400) reads: "The sages of bygone days regarded the *natya* (a dramatic presentation linking song, dance, mime, speech and scenery) as the offering most favored by the gods. This art owes its origins to the god Shiva himself, who, in his double role of Shiva-Parvati, bequeathed two kinds of natya to the world: the majestic and virile *uddhata* and the gentle and attractive *lasya*, which was more appropriate to the fair sex. Together these two varieties reflect nature and life in all its moods, whether peaceful, passionate or solemn; in fact, natya is the highest possible form of emotional expression. It is a means, and indeed the only one, of captiva-

65

ting the eyes and ears of an audience consisting of people of widely differing personalities and tastes."

From the 16th century onward, we find music developing rapidly at the courts of the Mongolian princes. Many of these rulers were men of great philosophical wisdom, with a real interest in the arts. The names of some of their musicians are still remembered today. Tansen, for instance, court musician to the famous Akbar (1556-1605), made one of the most successful attempts to fuse Hindu and Muslim musical styles. His mastery of the ancient Hindu vocal style, *Dhrupad,* with its noble simplicity, did not prevent him from creating a new genre, *Dabari,* which was subsequently regarded as being of the utmost perfection. The court historiographer, Abul Fazal, said of Tansen: "His melodies are so sweet and alluring that they can whirl the listener into a state of ecstasy or elevate him into a spiritual trance."

At the court of the emperor Mohammed Schah (1719-1748), contemporary with our Baroque era, another musical style appeared, known as *kheyal* (meaning "imagination"). This was characterized by decorative elements such as trills and tremolos, the use of ritardandos, and the considerable freedom it gave to the performer. It was created by Nyamat Khan, whose sovereign nicknamed him *Sadarang* ("always joyful").

In the same epoch, a type of music particularly associated with love songs arose, called *Thumre,* signifying "the graceful yet impatient stamping of feet".[53]

All these musical styles are used in India to this day.

The Future of Indian Music

India is developing more rapidly than ever before, and any attempt to assess her musical future must necessarily be premature. It is nonetheless ironical that in such countries as China and Japan, where until comparatively recently all contact with the Western world was deliberately eschewed, music has became closely attached to the European school, whereas in India the art still retains most of its inherited national characteristics.

51

66 *Puppets for a shadow theatre.*

Most Oriental countries have been subjected to Chinese, Hindu or Islamic influence, and their musical traditions have been duly affected. In many cases they have become so like their models as to be almost indistinguishable from them. There are national differences, of course, but these are so slight as to be of interest only to the specialist. The astonishing orchestral art of Bali merits special attention, however, both for its orginality and for its bearing on Western music at the turn of the 20th century. Although Bali came under the influence of the ancient Hindu culture, her instrumental music is more akin to the Chinese ritualistic style.

It is interesting that the Balinese have never felt the need to theorize about their art, which has consequently remained purely empirical. The respect these people feel for the divine origins of their music has precluded any attempt to change it, and the tradition continues today much as it has since time immemorial.

As in India, the music and ritual dances of Bali are associated with worship and the temple, and as such are performed as offerings to the gods.

Balinese music is focused on the *gamelan,* an orchestral form which, for sheer brilliance of sound and complexity of rhythm, is unique in musical history. The chief melody instrument is the *gambang kayu,* equivalent to our xylophone. The

53

keys, of varying lengths according to pitch (over a range of four octaves), are made of bronze, iron, wood or bamboo, and are attached to a sound box of wood or bamboo. Small tuned gongs also come into this category. Delicate figurations are woven round the principal melody by the flute and the *rebab* (a kind of violin with two strings).

The rhythmic refinement of Balinese music means that percussion instruments are important. They include cymbals, cone-shaped drums, and numerous gongs of various sizes. The instruments are often used in pairs, which are deliberately slightly mistuned to create a special jangling effect known as *tanguran,* giving added brilliance to the orchestral texture.[54]

Beside the ritual gamelan, several other types of ensemble exist; these are used to accompany Balinese dramatic presentations, such as the *gambuh* (a kind of opera), ceremonial functions and shadow plays.

The scores of Balinese orchestral music are based to a large extent on heterophonic treatment. The various instruments of the gamelan follow essentially the same melodic line but in varying degrees of rhythmic animation and melodic elaboration.

The scale generally used in Balinese music is pentatonic (five notes to the octave).

67

54

67-69 Javanese gong,
katjapi (kind of kithara) and
gambang kayu (a portable xylophone).
70-71 Chinese kitharas.

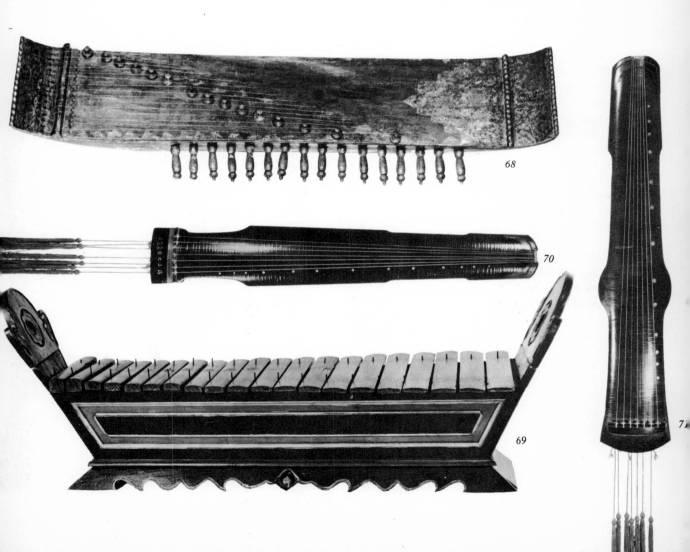

68

70

69

71

72 *Chart of a hand showing the 12 fundamental notes.*
73 *Deity praying to Buddha. Detail from a temple fresco. (Thailand)*

In China, civilization is not looked upon as a gift from the gods to be hallowed by philosophers, but as the creation of sages. "The prerequisites of any civilized society are that men should acquire wisdom and practice justice. The pathway to perfection lies in the collection of golden rules embodied in the rites." (Siun Tseu, 4th century B.C.) This compendium of rules, telling men how to behave in all circumstances, forms one of the constituents of etiquette, which in turn upholds the order of the universe. The other factor is music. "Music creates a harmonious union between heaven and earth; rites provoke good order in heaven and on earth. Perfection in music brings peace and morality; perfection in the rites puts an end to quarrels and rebellions."[55]

In all the great civilizations of the past, music occupies such a central position that its history is really also a chronicle of the relationship between man and the universe. Similarly, the true function of the scale has always been that of a ladder reaching from earth to heaven through the octave of the universe.

The tonal material on which Chinese music is based has been calculated according to strict mathematical principles, which, significantly, were invented not by musicians, but by astronomers, specialists in the art of numbers.

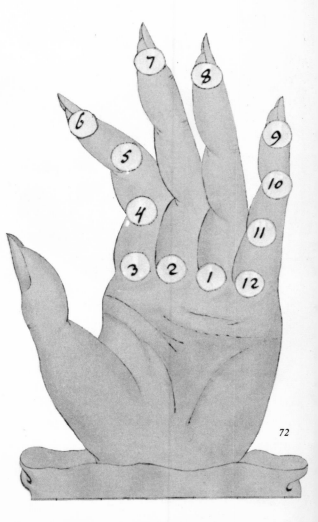

72

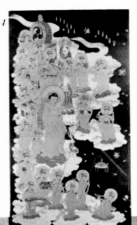

74-78 *Orchestral retinue of a god, with musicians playing the gong, flute, drum, kithara and lute. (Southeast Asia)*

75

76

77 78

79

80

79-82 *Chinese musicians.*
(17th or 18th century)
79 **San-hsien,** *a*
three-stringed guitar.
80 **Ta-sou-lo,** *a gong.*
81 **Ta-ta-lo,** *a gong.*
82 **Erl-hu,** *a kind*
of violin.

81

82

83-86 *Chinese musicians*
(see also 79-82).

83 *Cymbals.*

84 *Ten-note gong.*

85 *Transverse flute.*

86 *Trumpet.*

83

84

85

86

87 *Instrumental ensemble.*
(*from* **The Last Years of
the Life of Buddha—**
Thailand, 19th century)

The Chinese pentatonic scale is based on the notes produced by five bamboo pipes of carefully calculated lengths. Each note has various symbolical meanings: (1) *Kong,* the emperor, equivalent to the note f. This, the so-called yellow bell, is not only the principal note in music, but also the sacred foundation of the state and the people. (2) *Shang,* g, is the subjected people; it also represents the west, autumn and metal. (3) *Chiao,* a, the universe; also the east, spring and wood. (4) *Chi,* c′, the Prime Minister; also the south, summer and fire. (5) *Yu,* d′, the affairs of state; also the north, winter and water.

To these notes the Emperor Wen, founder of the Chou dynasty (*ca.* 1000 B.C.), added two more. Only the original five were considered to be pure, however, and as any of these could be called the "principal," five different scales or modes were possible. Also, the fundamental note was movable to conform with the twelve months of the year, which meant that each set of five-note scales could be transposed, making sixty in all. Traditionally, the twelve tubes were arranged in a circular pattern to form a compass, so that the chief "yellow" tube pointed northward to the Land of the Dead (which, paradoxically, was also a reservoir of life).

The tubes were also divided into two groups of six, associated respectively with Yang and Yin, the opposing masculine and feminine elements in the universe.

Similar numerical symbolism was applied to architecture. Furthermore, the Chinese established a subtle relationship between music, food and flavor.[56]

Music in Society

In the Celestial Empire of China, every action and feeling was governed by the laws of etiquette. "If man deviates from the rites for only an instant, he will cause cruelty and arrogance in the world. If he diverges from the rules of music, he will bring licentiousness and perversion to his peoples," writes M. Granet. Even the way in which he laughed or cried was controlled to the finest degree.

In a society where such extreme importance was attached to the union between man and the universe, and where there was such an intimate communion with nature, it is not surprising that there should have been elaborate festivals to celebrate the passing of the seasons. These festivals generally took place in the spring and autumn, their purpose being to renew the bonds of harmony between man and the world, or, more specifically, to symbolize the union between the two polar forces, Yang and Yin. The outstanding feature of the ceremonies was

88 *Chinese manuscript of musical notation. (from the 8th century)*

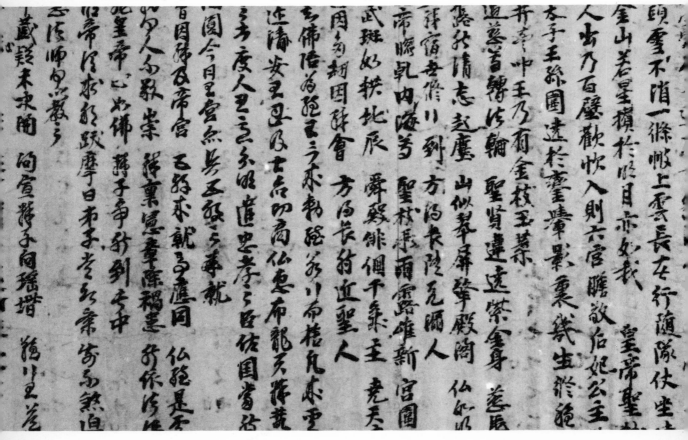

66

the singing and dancing, in which choirs of boys and girls sang antiphonally with stylized gestures representing the movements of animals or flowers. (According to M. Granet, this tradition goes back to the ancient court dances, one of which symbolized flowers and branches swaying in the wind. "Her body is an autumn iris nodding in the breeze," said Houai-nan Tsen in describing a dancer.) These dances, sometimes slow and sinuous, sometimes fast and energetic, were accompanied by the music of clay tambourines and choirs evoking thunder and rushing waters. The poems (in the form of a sequence of couplets) also varied in mood, from the jerky, breathless rhythms of the *fou* to the regular, tranquil couplets of the *che king*.

Chinese poetry has always been inseparable from song. A passage from a treatise called "Yo-Ki" ("Memorial to Music"), said to be edited by Confucius (551-479 B.C.), illustrates this point: "Song is a kind of speech, indeed, it is an extension of it. The natural expression of joy is speech. When the emotion is particularly strong, words alone cannot express it, and so speech is imperceptibly transformed into song. This inspires a feeling of ecstasy in which bodily movement is inevitable; hand and foot gestures gradually blossom into dancing." (After Ma Hiao-tsium.)

Sometimes the fou was used as a poetic accompaniment to religious ceremonies, at which the souls of the dead were invoked to act as a medium between man and the spiritual world. The priestesses danced, "naked and perfumed, flower in hand, seducing and capturing the souls of their ancestors; one after another the dancers whirled round giddily, until exhausted by their spiritual burden, they yielded up flower and soul and fell swooning to the ground. In a small, closed antechamber priests crowded together, listening to the celestial voices rising to heaven; in the background drum-rolls could be heard, with the clangorous accompaniment of sweet-toned kitharas and shrill flutes."[57] Yet again we see music being used to provoke a state of ecstasy. In China, however, these orgiastic dances and sacred carousals were strictly disciplined, in accordance with traditional codes of behavior.

Music played an important part in Chinese secular life, too. Just as the feudal lords of the Middle Ages received minstrels and troubadours into their castles to entertain them, so the Chinese princes and potentates hired jesters, dancers, epic poets, musicians and puppet theatre groups. Throughout the ages these performers kept alive the rich treasury of legends and traditional arts of the distant past.

As music was reputed to have such a profound

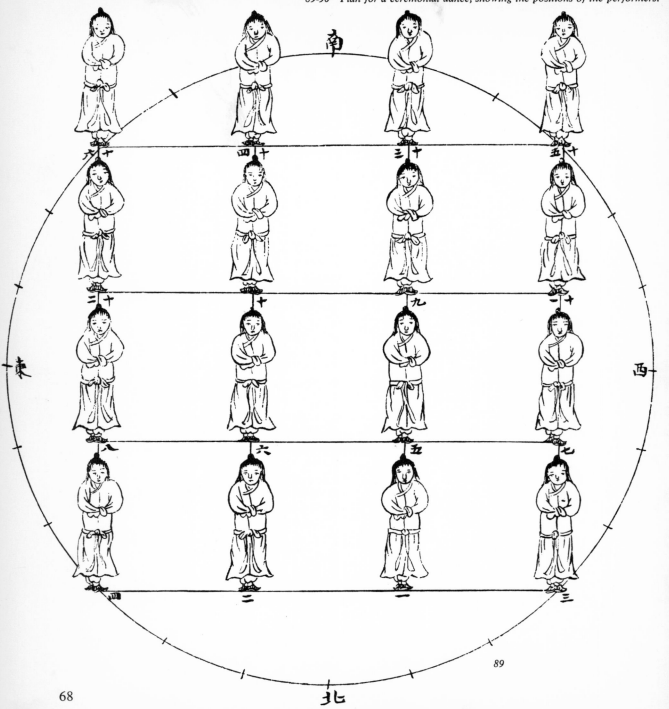

89-90 *Plan for a ceremonial dance, showing the positions of the performers.*

89

68

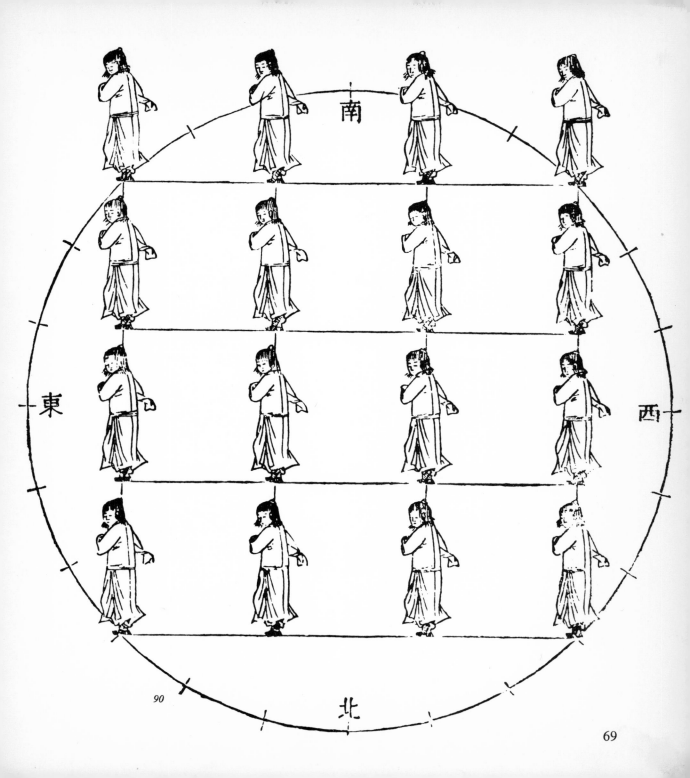

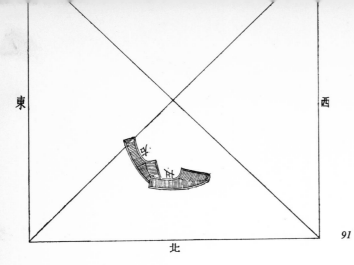

東　　　西

北

effect on cosmic and social life, it is not surprising that each sovereign had his own musical system, devised under his authority if not actually by him. (This did not prevent court historiographers, however, from keeping a careful account of the musical legacy of previous dynasties.) Eventually, there was a true break with the past. In the 4th and 5th centuries B.C., an *ars nova* arose in opposition to the traditional musical style, which suddenly seemed a trifle dull (if not downright tedious, according to some authors). The old style was later restored by the Emperor Wu Ti (141-87 B.C.), who considered that the *ars nova* was having a harmful influence on public morals. (Who knows what pernicious effects our atonal music will have on us?) Wu Ti also founded an Imperial Institute of Music, for establishing a collection of national music, for supervising rites and ceremonies, and for standardizing pitch (by means of the bamboo tubes described earlier).

Music at court reached its apotheosis during the Chou dynasty (1027-256 B.C.), when the number of musicians in the royal service reached nearly fifteen hundred. Court entertainments were wonderful to behold. They included enormous instrumental ensembles, meticulously divided into groups according to tone-color; stylized ballets, in which every detail was finely calculated; and innumerable poems and songs, which were either commissioned for the occasion to poets and bards, or taken from the collection of odes that Confucius had reportedly saved from oblivion in the 5th century B.C. It was the custom during the Chou dynasty for these court ceremonies to reflect the various seasons, and so the music had to be in perfect accord with the rhythm of nature. A different mode was used for each month of the year, the starting note depending on the position of the sun. (The "compass" of bamboo pipes was used in these calculations.)

China reached the zenith of her political and artistic power during the T'ang dynasty (7th to 10th centuries A.D.), when she was undoubtedly the most civilized country in the world. Virtuoso musicians from western countries (such as the Indies and Turkestan) were attracted to China, which was at that time wide open to foreign influences. There were ten main orchestras, each composed of a definite number of instrumentalists and dancers, and each devoted to the music of a certain country.

The first Chinese school of drama and music was established A.D. 714, with an enrollment of three hundred students.

The theatre in China developed slowly, however; it was not until the end of the 13th century, during the Mongolian-dominated Yuan dynasty,

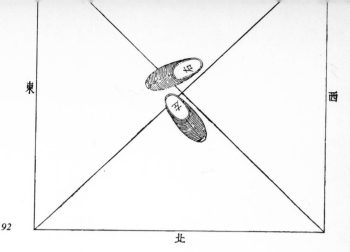

東

西

北

92

that it found the form in which it was to continue successfully until the present day. The type of entertainment that emerged was midway between music drama and opera, consisting of declamation, singing, instrumental music, dancing and pantomime. (Today acrobatics are included.)

The golden age of the Chinese Theatre lasted from the 13th to the 19th centuries. Originally, two distinct theatrical and musical styles were discernible. In the popular theatre of the northern provinces, only stringed instruments were used, tuned to the heptatonic (seven-note) scale; in the south a more literary style prevailed, with singing accompanied by the transverse flute, tuned to the pentatonic (five-note) scale. As time progressed, however, these styles gradually converged. About a century ago the classical theatre was supplanted by the *King-tiao* ("Theatre of Peking") which is of a popular nature and largely dependent on stage effects for its appeal. The orchestra, comprising strings and percussion, is more subordinate than in previous centuries, merely doubling the voice-part and adding brief interludes.[58]

Let us digress for a moment, and return to the Classical Age. In a delightful anecdote by M. Granet, we find the master of the royal music in the somewhat unexpected role of chief serenader to the Empress awaiting the birth of her child. Three

months before the confinement, he took up his position of honor on the left of her door, tuning fork in hand. "The chief steward (in his dual capacity of Prime Minister and head chef) was posted on the right, armed with a ladle. When the Empress called for music, however, her musician sometimes ran out of ideas, and so claiming to have confused the strings of his kithara, he refused to play. Similarly, when the Empress asked for food and the chief steward had nothing suitable prepared, he would plead that the dish was not fitting for the heir to the throne." At the baby's birth, and before his christening, the chief musician had to determine which five notes the baby cried on, and the chef had to discover which five flavors suited him.[59] The ingenuity of the Chinese is inexhaustible!

Instruments

Ancient Chinese treatises, including the "Record of Rites," edited according to tradition by Confucius, classify musical instruments according to the material from which they are made. We shall adopt the same procedure.

Metal: Free-hanging bronze bells (*to*) date from the 16th century B.C.; suspended bells (*chung*), hanging from a wooden stand in a series of sixteen

93 Kouei teaching music to the sons of princes and dignitaries

96

95

different sizes, date from the 11th century B.C. Together with the gong and the bronze drum, these instruments were used for military purposes and funeral rites.

Stone: Sonorous stones (*ch'ing*) are among the oldest Chinese instruments, and are often made of jade. Stone chimes (*pien ch'ing*) are suspended on a stand in groups of sixteen, like the bells described above.

Clay: The globular flute (*hun*) is equivalent to our ocarina; it is about the size and shape of a goose's egg, and is made of terra cotta or lacquered porcelain, with a number of finger holes and a mouthpiece. It was used particularly for popular music and, later, at court entertainments.

Skin: A large number of drums (*po fu*) come into this category. In battle, the sound of the drums was a sign of attack, just as the sound of the gong or bell indicated retreat. Sometimes the drums were daubed with the blood of the vanquished. In the orchestra, the drummer was looked upon as the leader.

Silk: The two instruments dating from the Classical era are the *k'in* (Chinese zither) and its variant the *shê*. The k'in has five or seven strings, and the shê, between seventeen and fifty. These are made of silk threads, and are capable of producing a wide variety of sonorities. The k'in is about eight inches wide and four feet long, while the shê, altogether larger, is about seven feet long.

It is interesting that the k'in was the favorite instrument of Chinese writers; it was treated as the point of departure for philosophical speculation, and has been the source of inspiration for countless beautiful poems. The sacred character attributed to the k'in meant that a purification ceremony had to be enacted before it could be played. The instrument was then set into position for performance on a little table specially designed for the purpose. It seems that the k'in was already in use as early as the 10th or 11th century B.C., but although the music written for the instrument always appealed to the Chinese intelligentsia, it was not generally appreciated until its full flowering some two thousand years later during the Ming dynasty (1368-1644). Still today one comes across skilled players of the k'in, which continues to be held in exceptionally high regard.

In the category of silk-stringed instruments we must also mention some later arrivals on the historical scene: the *p'i-p'a,* a kind of guitar of foreign origin, dating from the 3rd century B.C. and still popular today, and its variants, the three-stringed *san-hien,* the *jouan,* the *chou ang-ts'ing* and the *yue-k'in.*

74

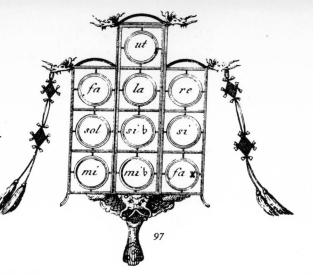

95 Kuan, a Chinese chalumeau; in this case, a double-reeded instrument, and the ancestor of the oboe.
96 Tchang-Kou, a drum in the shape of an hourglass.
97 Yun-lo, a type of gong played in both temple and palace.
98 Hsiao, an ancient Chinese flute.

(these four illustrations from an essay on music by La Borde and Roussier, Paris, 1780)

97

All these instruments were plucked. The Chinese also possessed various kinds of violin, however, generally with two strings, called the *hou-k'in, eul-hou* and *king-hou,* the last being a miniature version with a shrill tone.

Wood: Two percussion instruments come under this heading, the *chφu* and the *yu.* The *chφu* took form of a square trough, eighteen inches deep; this was hit with a wooden hammer to announce the beginning of a ceremony, a hymn, or even a single verse. The yu was fashioned in the shape of a recumbent tiger (a foot high and just over two feet long), whose spine was serrated with twenty-seven notches; a split bamboo stick was rubbed along this three times to indicate the end of the performance. Also made of wood are two double-reeded wind instruments of a more recent date: the *kouan,* with seven or eight holes (used in the 6th century), and the *sona,* the Chinese oboe, which dates from the 16th century and is still popular today.

Gourd: The empty rind of the gourd was used to make the *sheng,* a kind of mouth organ. A number of bamboo pipes (twelve to seventeen) were stuck into the gourd, in the side of which was a mouthpiece. Each pipe had a reed and a finger hole, and by covering these holes different notes could be sounded simultaneously.

Bamboo: Panpipes and transverse and vertical flutes come into this group. Incidentally, there is no known written record of music for any instruments except the k'in before the T'ang dynasty (A.D. 618-907).[60]

Assimilation of Western Music

It was not until the early years of the 20th century that the Chinese public at large became acquainted with Western music. The first symphony orchestra was founded by foreigners at Shanghai before the First World War, and this gave the Chinese an opportunity to hear classical and modern masterpieces of the West. In 1927, the first conservatory of music was established in Shanghai. Since then Chinese composers have gradually assimilated Western musical styles, both in writing for the modern symphony orchestra and for their own traditional instruments.

98

99 *Japanese nobleman playing the transverse flute and being attacked by a bandit. (pen drawing)*
100 *Double tsouzoumi, an instrument made of two small drums mounted on a stick, which is shaken. Bells are often attached.*

The history of Japan falls conveniently into four periods. The first of these is based on legend, and as such cannot really be regarded as history. The second (A.D. 522 to 1603) is the Classical period, when Japan was helped by China and Korea to discover and to express her own particular genius. The third is the feudal era, during which the Japanese grew introspective and concentrated entirely on developing their own spiritual heritage. The final period marks a complete reversal, with the Japanese deliberately trying to make contact with the Western world.

Although the first period has no direct bearing on the history of music, its delightful legends do at least show that music was practiced at this time. One story tells of how, at the inauguration of a palace in the 5th century, the Emperor Inkyo would make the Empress dance and play the *wagon* (the Japanese kithara). Another relates that at the death of this music-loving Emperor twenty Korean musicians working in Japan performed at his funeral. These players taught their Japanese colleagues Korean, Chinese and Indian musical methods and new instrumental techniques.

Classical Japan owes a great spiritual and cultural debt to China; the Japanese adopted Confucianism, and Chinese forms of medicine, architecture, painting and music. Even Buddhism

100

101

reached Japan through the Celestial Empire, but the teachings of Compatissant gave this religion an entirely new and typically Japanese form, known as the Zen philosophy. A similar metamorphosis took place in the arts, including music. The Japanese took over the Chinese pentatonic scales and Chinese instruments dating from the Middle Empire period; in so doing they created an entirely original musical style, clearly distinguishable from its models by its pervading melancholy, especially in the haunting inflections of its melodic lines.

The Classical period was also the Golden Age of the *gagaku* (literally, "graceful music"), a genre borrowed from the Chinese court of the T'ang dynasty (A.D. 618-917). Although this elegant and highly organized art gradually became obsolete in China, it has been preserved virtually in its original form at the imperial court of Japan. Gagaku is essentially orchestral music, based on two pentatonic scales. Many different instruments are used, and the total sound effect is extraordinarily mellifluous—it has been compared with the gentle rustlings of nature.

The chief wind instruments are the *hichiriki,* the Japanese oboe, which generally play the principal melody, and the *ryuteki,* a wooden transverse

102

78

101 *Woman playing the kokyu,*
a small bowed shamisen.
102 *Players of the koto,*
the Japanese kithara, at a
concert in the house of a nobleman.
(School of Tosa, first half of
the 17th century)

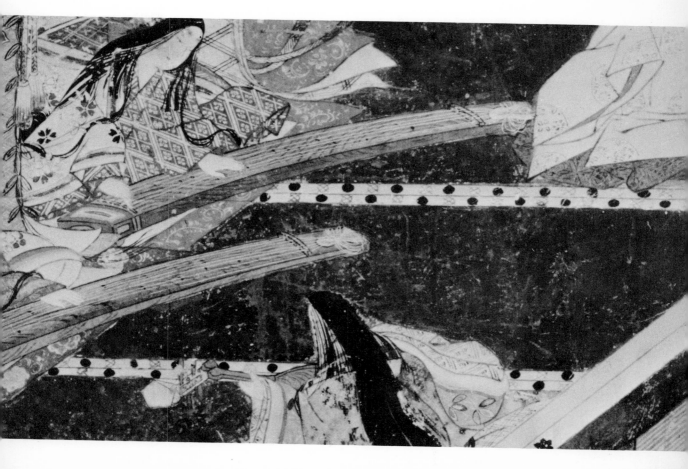

104

103

flute, which either doubles the hichiriki in unison or adds a decorated version of the tune. Also in this category comes the *sho,* a kind of mouth organ comprising seventeen slender bamboo pipes. As five or six notes can be sounded at once, this instrument provides the harmonic foundation of the orchestra. The harmony produced by the sho is not based on thirds, however, like our Western harmony, but on seconds, fourths and fifths. It is interesting that the harmonies used by Debussy are often similarly constructed—*Poissons d'Or,* for example. We know that Debussy heard and admired Oriental music, including the gagaku, at the World Exhibition in Paris in 1889.[61]

The most important stringed instruments are the *biwa* and the *koto*. The biwa is a kind of lute, of Asian origin; it has four strings, which are plucked with a plectrum. The koto is a large kithara, deriving from the Chinese *k'in*. There are two types: the older *yamato-koto,* or wagon, with six strings, and the *so-no-koto,* with thirteen; both are treated as rhythm instruments, the strings being plucked with ivory strips attached to the first three fingers of the right hand.

Percussion instruments include the *taiko* and *kakko* (kinds of drum) and the *shoko,* a metal gong.

105

106

Two instruments remain to be mentioned: the *shamisen* and the *shakuhachi,* both particularly characteristic of Japan. The shamisen is the favorite instrument of the geishas, who are renowned for their expertise in music, dancing and literature, as well as in the art of love. Like so many Japanese instruments, the shamisen is of Chinese origin; it was not known in Japan until the sixteenth century. Elegantly proportioned, with a long, slender neck (to which are attached three strings), a rather small body, and large, highly decorated pegs, this graceful instrument has become inseparable from the Japanese way of life. Finally, we come to the shakuhachi, which is an end-blown bamboo flute and essentially a solo instrument. Its tone-color is surprisingly rich and velvety, especially in the lower register.

The complexity of the gagaku was so great that A.D. 710 (at the beginning of the Japanese Golden Age), the Emperor Temmu appointed a musical director to train the court musicians. These numbered 254 in all, including men and women singers, instrumentalists, teachers and students. In addition, there were thirty masters and 120 pupils from China and Korea. These figures are sufficient proof of the lively interest taken in the arts in court circles.

In the middle of the 9th century music underwent a reform whereby all foreign influences were consciously eliminated and stress was placed instead on the national characteristics of the art. Court musicians were exempted from all taxes, and the profession became strictly hereditary, a tradition that continues today.

Besides the gagaku, one of the most original Japanese art forms is the *nô.* This dramatic genre emerged in the 14th century, having sprung originally from the *kagura,* a religious dance. In many ways the nô is similar to ancient Greek tragedy, with its declamatory incantations, its masks and sumptuous costumes, its slow and stylized choreography, and its unison choirs accompanied by a single flute and two drums.

As in China, Japanese poetry is closely linked with music and mime; the performers often accompany themselves with instruments, especially the shamisen, the koto and the flute.

Modern Japan has deliberately exposed herself to the influence of Western music and instruments. Indeed, Japanese pianists number among some of the most outstanding interpreters of the classical repertoire. Avant-garde music has also found many skillful exponents, especially in the field of electronic music.

81

107 *Musician playing the tounbour, the Persian lute.*
108 *Persian dancer.*

107

108

The music of Persia and the music of Islamic Arabia have a common origin and date from the Sassanid dynasty (A.D. 224 to 641). In the 7th century B.C. vocal and instrumental music existed in Persia, but we know little about it other than that it played an important part in the religious and social life of the people. When the Arabs invaded and took possession of Persia in the 7th century A.D., they found there a level of culture infinitely superior to their own. Music was no exception. The Arabs quite shamelessly based their musical theory on Iranian scale systems and adopted Persian instruments, which were of a more sophisticated design than theirs. The most popular of these was the lute; others included the *tounbour* (a long-necked mandolin), the *mizaf* (a twelve-stringed kithara), the flute and the tambourine.

The scale system taken over by the Arabs from the Persians in this Islamic period was not unlike that used in India. The octave was divided into either seventeen or twenty-two microtonal intervals (Arab theorists disagree on the exact number), which may be compared with the twenty-two Hindu *srutis*.

These notes formed the basis of a series of twelve primary modes called *maqamats*, from which were derived a large number of subsidiary modes. Again we are reminded of the Hindu raga system.

From a purely historical point of view, the importance of these Persian modes adopted by the Arabs cannot be overestimated, as they formed the basis of music throughout the entire Muslim world, from Bagdad to Seville. (This does not mean to say, of course, that the mode-forms were impervious to local influences.)

It is worth noting, too, that as time went on the Arabs amplified their theoretical knowledge by borrowing freely from the musical treatises of Greek thinkers. Gradually the Arabs outstripped the Greeks, developing philosophical and musical theories of their own; the most outstanding of these appear in 10th-century treatises by Al-Farabi and Avicenna.

Under the Abassid Caliphs (750-847), especially Harun-al-Rachid (of *A Thousand and One Nights* fame), Bagdad became the center of artistic activity in the Arabic world, just as previously its neighbor Babylon had been the model for the Mediterranean kingdoms. Rarely has a society shown such a partiality for poetry linked with music as that of 9th-century Bagdad. Some of the musical forms created in this era are used in Arab countries today.

Despite this wonderful flowering of secular music, Islamic religious music was strictly limited in scope. Instruments could be used only at special family celebrations, such as a wedding. Otherwise music was banned from worship, except for the chanting of the call to prayer and the chanting of the sacred Koran. As a consequence, instrumental music was slow in developing, and vocal music was confined to monody, suitable for the chants mentioned above and for the recitation of the works of the great Persian poets. In this particular genre, however, the melodic refinement and subtlety of expression that were achieved are again reminiscent of the ragas of Northern India. Despite the somewhat contradictory pronouncements on music by the prophet Mohammed, the Arabs showed a true passion for the art. Minstrels and bards were engaged at court, many of them skilled in poetry, singing, instrumental playing and composing, and it was quite usual for the rich to employ harems of singers and dancers.

Eventually the Arabs accepted music even in their religion, and the various cults of dancing dervishes practiced *sama* ("hearing") and used music to great advantage to bring about the state of musical ecstasy or trance.

110

The Wonderful World
of Oriental Instruments

111 Korean drum.
112 Big Chinese gong in bronze and brass.
113-114 Two views of a Chinese ocarina, showing
four and two holes respectively.
115 Chinese flute with five holes.
116 Idiophones designed to dispel evil spirits.
117 Bronze temple gong. (Borneo)
118 Chinese bronze bell and two small
Japanese bells.
119 Ornamental conch. (Tibet)
120 Tibetan copper horn decorated with silver.
121 Chinese or Tibetan chalumeau. (20th century)
122 Japanese chime bells.
123 Tibetan copper horn.
124 Sarinda, an Indian stringed instrument.
125 Japanese kithara.
126 Indian setar. (20th century)
127 Sarinda, a bowed instrument. (Bengal)
128 Rebab, a bowed instrument (Persia)
129 Persian instrument similar to the lute.
130 Rebab (Malayan vielle). (Java)

131 *Persian kemange, with seven strings.*

132 *Temple gong in bronze. (Borneo)*

133 *Chinese wooden instrument in the form of a recumbent tiger. Its serrated back is rubbed with a bamboo stick.*

134 *Picture of an ancient Chinese bell, painted on silk.*

135 *Chinese mounted drum.*

136 *Sheng, a Chinese mouth organ. This generic title covers several varieties, which differ according to the number of pipes they have—from seven to 36.*

137 *Tchoung: an assortment of suspended bells from the 18th century, equivalent to the Pien-Tchoung of ancient music.*

138 *Chinese lithophones. (18th century)*

139-146 *Various Chinese instruments: drums, bells, gongs, a carillon with steel chime-blocks, and a lithophone with suspended jade blocks. (Figures 137 through 146 are taken from the treatise on music by La Borde and Roussier, Paris, 1780)*

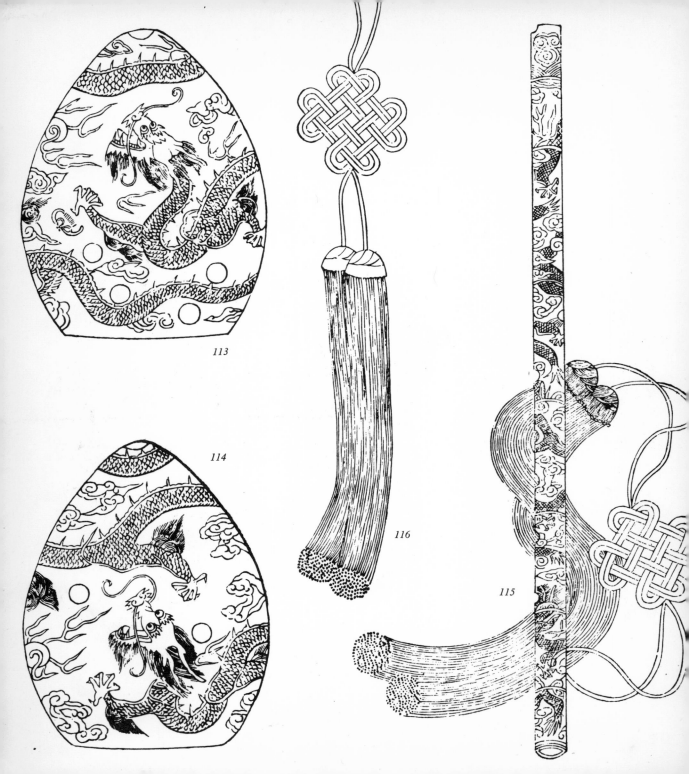

113

114

116

115

117

120   121   122

123   124   125

126   127   12

129   130   131

132

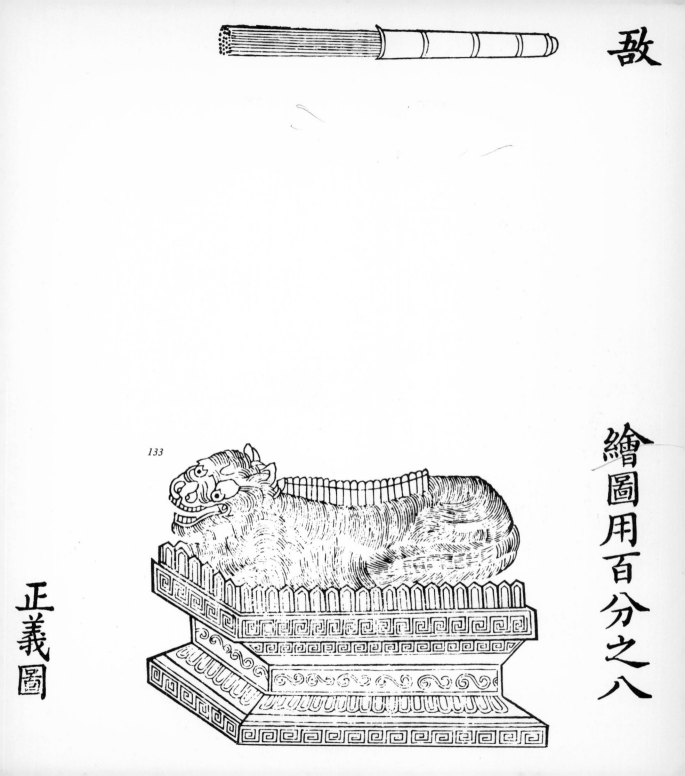

繪圖用百分之八

正義圖

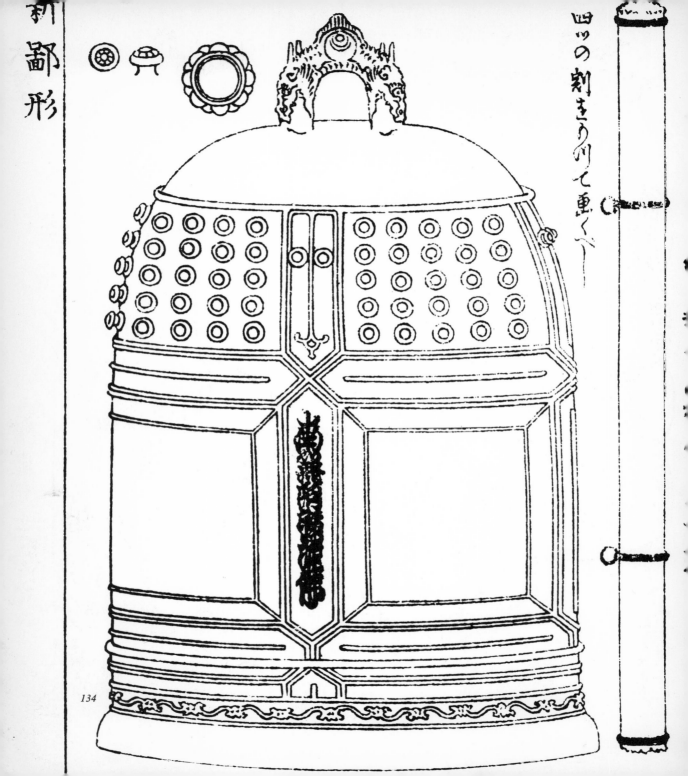

四ツの割きり川て重くべ一

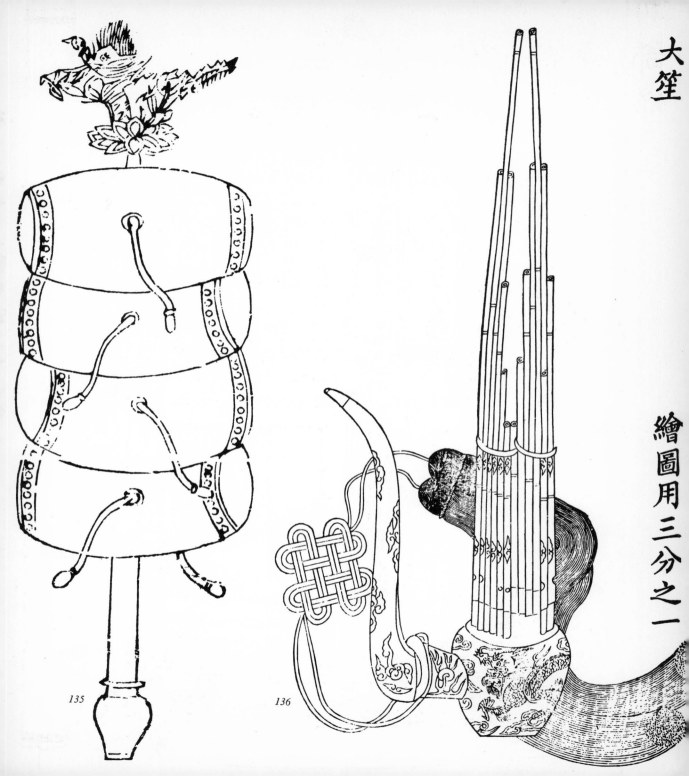

大笙

繪圖用三分之一

135

136

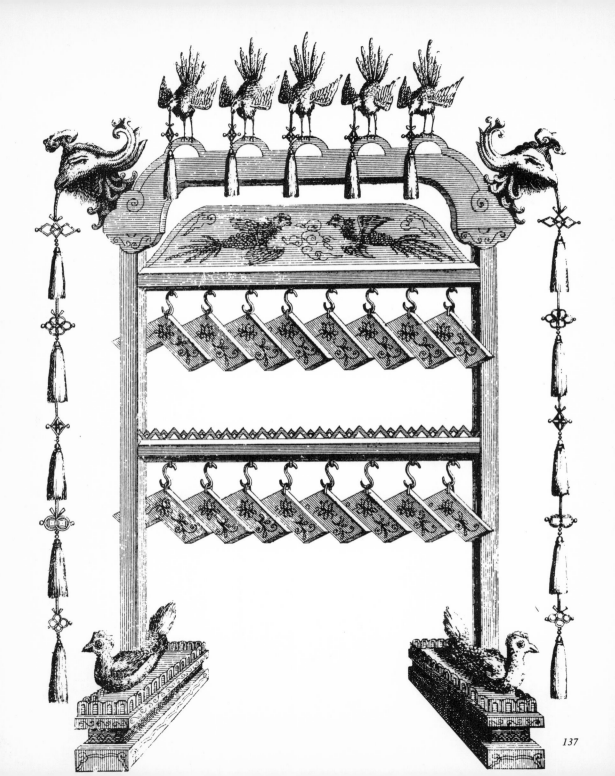

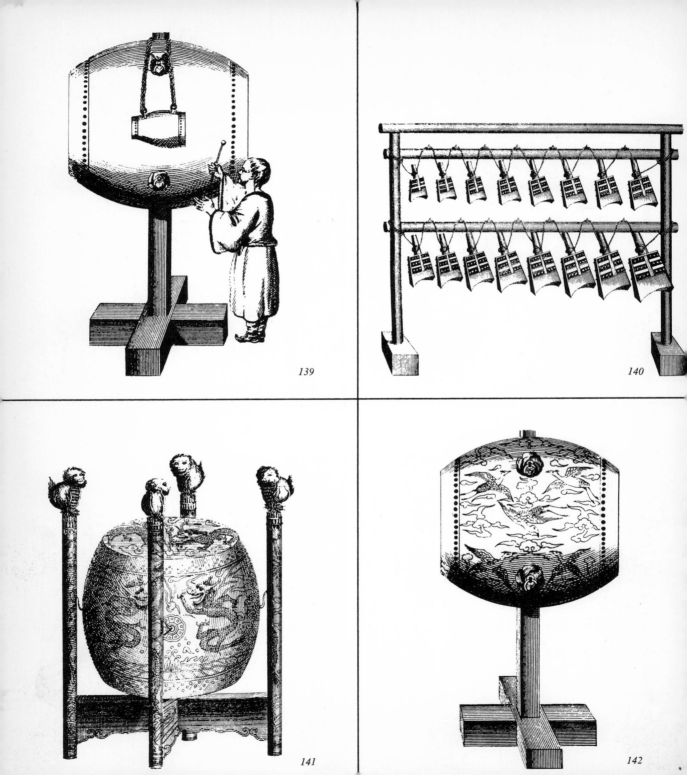

139

140

141

142

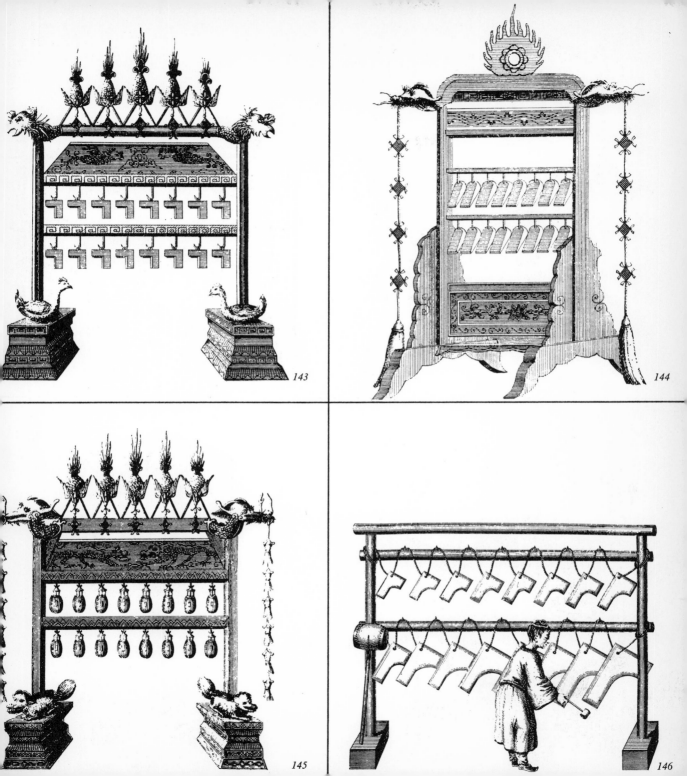

143

144

145

146

147 *Lyre player. (Ancient Greece)*
148 *Boetian statuette in the form of a bell. (Thebes—ca. 700 B.C.)*

"Every one of us should regard the bards and epic poets with the utmost respect. They are the favorites of the muses, who inspire them to write their masterpieces." Thus proclaimed Ulysses in the land of the Phaeacians (Book Eight of Homer's *Odyssey*).

In ancient times the bard took his place beside the priest, soothsayer and prophet in the performance of rites to maintain a harmonious relationship between man and the gods. "The task of the first bards was to conserve the rules of the sacred prosody which accompanied the strictly disciplined ritual dances."[62]

As time went on, the severe yoke of religion imposed on the bards was relaxed. The epic poem, originally based on sacred subjects, became secularized. Nevertheless, the time-honored prestige of the bard lived on; he retained the emblem of his profession—the sceptre—and continued to wear the long robe otherwise reserved for priests. For hours on end he would declaim his poetry with a passionate intensity, accompanying himself on the kithara. (It is interesting that the bards, like the Egyptian harpists, were often blind.)

Plato claimed in his *Republic* that the slightest change in the science of music would upset the moral welfare of the entire State. Pythagoras believed that the heavenly bodies themselves were

151

152

153

governed by numerical laws based on music. It is hardly surprising, then, that the teaching of music had precedence over literature, and that it was considered essential for everyone to learn how to sing and to play an instrument. Plutarch tells us that he felt his education was lacking because he had not mastered the art of playing the kithara.[63]

The kithara, an elaborate version of the lyre, was the sacred instrument of Apollo and the favorite stringed instrument of the Ancient Greeks. It is depicted countless times in the musical scenes decorating Greek vases. The concert kithara was often intricately embellished, and the sound box was laminated inside to increase the volume of sound. The strings were plucked either with a plectrum or with the fingers. Besides various kinds of kithara, the Greeks also used a stringed instrument similar in shape to our triangular harp. No bowed instruments were known at this time.

Other vase paintings show scenes in which a music master, seated on a throne-like chair, is teaching a group of children, sitting on low stools, to play the kithara or the aulos. "Sometimes the master is singing or playing the kithara, while his pupil, facing him, accompanies him on the aulos."[64]

The use of the aulos was as widespread in the ancient world as that of the lyre and the kithara. Although the term "aulos" is sometimes used loosely to include reedless instruments of the flute family, strictly speaking it is a wind instrument with either a single reed and cylindrical bore, or a double reed and conical bore (the ancestor of the clarinet and oboe, respectively). The double aulos had two pipes, one serving as a drone. According to legend, the aulos was dedicated to Dionysus; it was thus associated with orgiastic music, and as such was the special instrument of the courtesans, who also played the tambourine, the cymbals, the sistrum and the krotala.[65] Brass instruments were relegated to military use.

The musical education of a child in Ancient Greece was not complete without the study of the kindred arts, dancing and mime. Indeed, music, poetry and dance were closely allied at this time, as they were throughout the ancient Eastern world. Music in education was of paramount importance, even in Sparta, with its famous military schools. "The constant practice of music and dancing," writes O. Tiby, "alleviated the harshness of the educational regime . . . the Spartan army marched to war to the sound of the aulos, and sang as they attacked the enemy . . . and thanked the gods for their victory in a paean of song. To be able to hold one's part in a choir was one of the disciplines of a Spartan citizen." At Athens, children's choirs participated in the many annual religious and civic

108

154

festivals. After the battle of Salamis, in 480 B.C., Sophocles, then a man of fifty, "naked and anointed with oil, lyre in hand, conducted a choir of children in a song of victory."[66]

The adult members of the Athenian community took part as singers and dancers in the dramatic representations held to celebrate the Festival of Dionysus. These versatile performers were chosen and trained by musical directors, who were in turn selected by the city magistrates. Every city of any importance boasted an amphitheatre; this was looked upon, not as a secular institution, but as having the sacred character of a temple. The priest of Dionysus and a statue of the god were always present at the dramatic representations given there.

The Festival of Dionysus itself lasted four days, with nonstop performances of fifteen or sixteen tragedies and comedies—something like twenty thousand verses of spoken or sung poetry, not to mention the opening ceremonial dithyrambs. Quite a feat of endurance for the Greek theatregoing public![67]

The cult of Apollo, the chief muse, was even more definitely musically orientated. The ceremonies held in his honor were an excuse for great competitive festivals between singers, kithara players, poets, rhapsodes, children's choirs and adult choirs—particularly at Delos, Delphi, Sparta and Athens. Some of the winning singers and instrumentalists remained famous in Greece centuries later.

What was this music like, we wonder, and what rules did it follow?

It must be emphasized that Greek choral and instrumental music was essentially monodic. Any effects of heterophony were incidental rather than a deliberate attempt to create a richer texture, and, as in India and China, polyphony as such was unknown.

Greek monodic music was based on the *nomoi* (literally, "laws"). These were traditional melodies which, like the Indian raga and the Arabic maqamat, formed the basic structure for improvisation. It was the performer's task to choose the melodic formula suitable for each occasion, and to decorate it accordingly. How was this suitability assessed? Whereas the Hindus and Arabs linked their ragas and maqamats with certain psychological or emotional states, the Greeks tended to associate the nomoi with pictorial or literary images. This is not really surprising when one considers that the Greeks were the originators of tragic drama and the creators of some of the world's finest statuary. Often a nomos was a sound-picture of an episode in the life of a god (for instance, the combat between Perseus and the gorgon, or be-

109

tween Apollo and the python); the nomos has been likened to a symphonic poem in miniature.

Besides the nomoi and epic poems sung by the bards, mention must be made of the banqueting song. The Greeks, like all the peoples of the ancient world, enjoyed music with their meals. (These banquets also gave rise to a special literary form, illustrated in the works of Plato and Plutarch, among others). The presence of a female oboist seems to have been obligatory at these all-male banquets; sometimes an acrobatic dancer would also perform.

The 7th century B.C. saw the rise of lyric poetry, including the love song, which Plato later called the tenth muse. It was intimate in style, the words and music being conceived together to be sung in recitative. This genre reached its highest level of refinement among the poet-musicians (Sappho and Alcaeus, for example) of the island of Lesbos.

The favorite music of the populace was undoubtedly choral singing. The citizens sang hymns (in praise or invocation to the gods); paeans (majestic victory songs); hyporchemata (lively dance-songs of Cretan origin); parthenia (wedding hymns); threnos (funeral dirges); and dithyrambs (wild Bacchanalian songs calculated to provoke a state of spiritual exaltation; later the dithyramb gave rise to Greek tragic drama).

156

157

Gradually choral music became more complicated, until eventually only professional choirs could perform it. The ancient strophic verse was superseded by a form that developed organically, giving greater scope for musical variety (in melody, rhythm, use of modes and chromaticism). One of the greatest composers of choral music was the poet-musician Pindar (*ca.* 518-438 B.C.).

With the rise of Greek tragedy, music continued to play an important part. The poetry was either spoken or sung, and the melody was conditioned by the natural stress and inflection of the words. The recitations, songs and choruses were generally accompanied by an aulos.

Greek Theory and the Modes

The Greeks recognized a theoretical division of the octave into twenty-four parts. Seven notes were chosen, each of which could be the starting point of a descending scale, mode or "harmonia." These modes were named after certain areas in Asia Minor—Dorian, Phrygian, Lydian, for example. The notes were carefully selected so that the top four formed the same pattern of intervals as the bottom four (the eighth note being a repetition an octave lower of the first). Each of these patterns was called a tetrachord, as it comprised three

intervals.[68] The top and bottom notes of each tetrachord were fixed, spanning a perfect fourth but the intervals in between were variable. In modern notation the three different "genera" of a tetrachord starting on E would be as follows:

Diatonic: E, D, C, B.

Chromatic: E, C♯, C, B.

Enharmonic: E, C, a note between C and B, B.

The Greeks believed that each mode possessed a particular ethical quality or *ethos,* and that the use of an unsuitable mode could upset the social order of the State. As illustrations, the Dorian mode was calming; the Phrygian, war-like; and the Lydian, soul-stirring.

In the 6th century B.C., Pythagoras and his followers began to write voluminously on such speculative subjects as the mystical significance of numbers and the harmony of the spheres. These treatises have held an extraordinary fascination for theorists from the Middle Ages onwards, but unfortunately they do not bring us any nearer to the actual music of Ancient Greece.

Perhaps, however, we need not regret the almost total lack of documentary evidence of Greek music. Alfred Einstein[69] believed that it is just as well that the fragmentary examples we do possess were discovered only in comparatively recent times. Com-

158

osers from the Middle Ages to the time of Wagner have been inspired, not by Ancient Greek music self, but by their own idealized conceptions of it. n short, ignorance has been the prime creator of some of our greatest masterpieces, especially in the realm of opera.

After the Roman Conquest

From the beginning of the Roman Conquest (*ca.* 200 B.C.), music showed a gradual but steady decline. It was not that the Romans disliked music —on the contrary, music was used a great deal in Rome— but whereas the Athenian nobleman had been proud to sing and dance in the chorus of a Greek dramatic presentation, conscious that he was carrying out a civic duty, the upper-class Roman felt it was beneath his dignity to appear in public as a performing musician, and relegated the practice of music to his slaves.

Despite the low social standing of musicians, some managed to win fame and fortune, especially the mummers, who performed in the new popular form of entertainment, the pantomime. This amounted to a kind of variety show, and its attraction for Roman audiences was so great that it soon completely replaced the classical tragic drama.

Mummers and virtuoso kithara players under-

took grand tours of the Roman Empire, thus spreading their fame abroad. Wherever they went they were mobbed by ardent fans, who would collect the plectra that their favorite players had used to pluck the strings of their instruments.

At the lavish gladiatorial shows held in Rome, the public heard the hydraulic organ, imported from Alexandria, noisy brass ensembles (of Etruscan origin) and instruments inherited from the Greeks or appropriated from other conquered nations.

In its transference from the Greek literati to the Roman populace, music lost much of its ethical character, and became for the first time simply an entertainment for the masses. A kind of pop culture developed, which—despite its universal appeal —showed a considerable lack of true creative imagination.

A group of reactionary musicians tried to recreate the monodic vocal style of the Greeks by setting to music the great Latin poetry of Catullus, Horace and Tibullus. The very essence of Greek monody lay in the simultaneous creation of the poetry and music, and so these laudable but artificial attempts failed to prevent the inevitable break between the two arts.

The decline continued, despite a sudden rage for

music among the upper classes in the 1st century A.D. It became the vogue for the elite to give concert tours throughout the Empire; Nero himself traveled to Greece to display his talents as a singer and as a player of the kithara and the *utricularius,* a kind of bagpipe. The Roman public cannot be blamed for its deteriorating musical taste, however, when even such renowned figures as Petronius appreciated only the lascivious aspect of music.

How surprised these imperial mountebanks would have been had they suspected that beneath the very paving stones of their own city, in the secrecy of the catacombs, a new musical style was germinating in the liturgical chanting of the persecuted Christians.

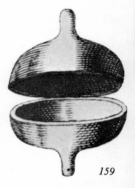

159

Conclusion

Perhaps the most impressive feature of ancient and Oriental music is the integral part it played in the life of the people. For thousands of years it served as a vital link between men and the gods. Today the art has become so commercialized that it is little more than a pleasant accessory to our day-to-day existence.

In view of this complete reversal of musical ideals, it is paradoxical that the mystical grandeur

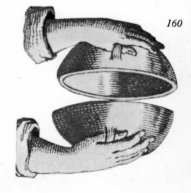

160

114

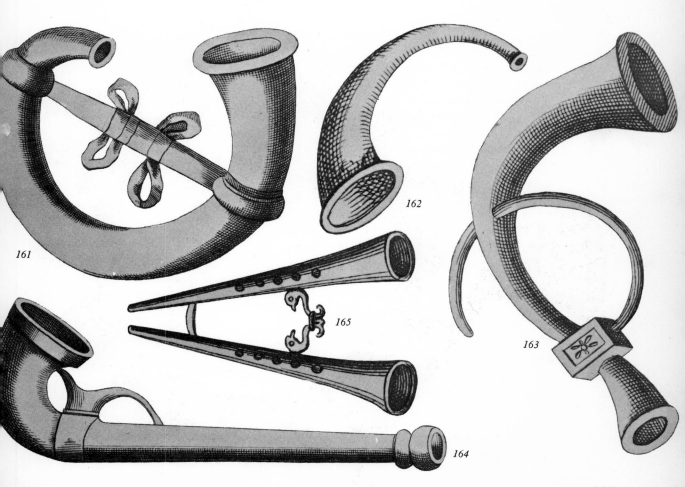

162

161

165

163

164

166-168 *Horns from Alexandria.*
(from Kirchner's Musurgia
Universalis, *Rome, 1650)*

166

167

168

117

of the concepts of ancient musicians was not fully realized in purely musical terms until the last four hundred years or so.

The inexorable rhythm of the universe pulsates in the concertos of Bach. The dances of the muses of Apollo and the shepherds of Krishna are immortalized in the music of Mozart. The moral and ethical power attributed to music by the ancient philosophers is unleashed in the symphonies of Beethoven. The mysterious communion of the soul with nature that the Hindus and Arabs sought in their improvisations on the *ragas* and *maqamats* is consummated in the works of Schubert, Schumann, Brahms and Debussy.

Today we are faced with an ever-increasing gap between the rich spiritual world of the creative artist and the pervading uniformity of everyday life. Religious festivals and ceremony in general have faded into the background, with the result that music, too, has lost its central position. We cannot fail to be struck by the irony of the situation. Ancient music, for all its technical limitations, was a spiritual necessity for the people, and so permeated their lives. The music of our great Western composers transcends even the noblest theoretical concepts of earlier civilizations, and yet modern materialism has relegated it to the level of a luxury for the enlightened few.

169 *The final dance of* Comus, *a masque by John Milton. (17th century engraving)*

Notes

1   The ideas developed in the first chapter owe a great deal to Walter Wiora's study, The Four Ages of Music; Kohlhammer, Stuttgart, 1961.
2   The importance of music's role is affirmed not only by Marius Schneider, but also by W. Wiora and Professor H. Kühn, an eminent author on prehistory.
3   Marius Schneider, Encyclopedia of the Pleiades: History of Music, Vol. I; Gallimard, 1960.
4   Marius Schneider, op. cit.
5   Mircea Eliade, Shamanism; Payot, Paris, 1951.
6-7   Marius Schneider, op. cit.
8   H. Kirchmeyer, The New Musical Journal, April, 1961.
9   Marius Schneider, op. cit.
10   Gilbert Rouget, Encyclopedia of the Pleiades, op. cit.
11   W. Wiora, op. cit.
12   G. Rouget, op. cit.
13-14   W. Wiora, op. cit.
15-16   S. N. Kramer, History Begins in Sumeria; Arthaud, 1957.
17   Quoted by W. Wiora, op. cit.
18   Jean Bottéro, Preface to the above work by S. N. Kramer.
19   Pierre Montet, Everyday Life in Egypt; Hachette.
20   Will Durant, The Story of Civilization, Vol. I.
21   A. Machabey, "Music and Mysticism," Musica, 1954, No. 5; Claude Frissard, "Musical Life in Ancient Mesopotamia," Musica, 1954, No. 11; "Musical Life in Ancient Israel," Musica, 1956, No. 9.
22   Will Durant, op. cit.
23   S. N. Kramer, op. cit.
24   Musica, 1954, No. 11.
25   Will Durant, op. cit.
26   J. Evola, The Metaphysics of Sex; Payot, Paris, 1959.
27   Will Durant, op. cit.
28   Hans Engel, Music and Society; Max Hesse, Berlin, 1960.
29   J. H. Breasted, History of Egypt; Phaidon, Zurich, 1954.
30   Hans Engel, op. cit.
31   W. Wiora, op. cit.
32   F. Behn, Musical Life in Antiquity and the Early Middle Ages, 1954.
33   Encyclopedia of the Pleiades and Music Past and Present; Barenreiter.
34   Encyclopedia of the Pleiades, op. cit.
35   See the works of E. M. von Hornbostel, Curt Sachs, M. Wegner, H. Hickmann.
36   Music Past and Present.
37   C. R. Srinivasa Aiyangar, "Looking at India"; Cahiers du Sud, Marseille, 1941.
38   Max-Pol Fouchet, The Art of Love in India; Guilde du Livre, Lausanne, 1957.
39   The Natyacastra of Bharata (ca. 200 B.C.), The Samgita Ratnakara of Sharngaveda (13th century), The Ragha Vibodha of Soma Nätha (17th century).
40   Ascending, unlike the descending seven-note scale.
41   Encyclopedia of the Pleiades, op. cit.
42   Cf. our scale system, which divides the octave into twelve semitones.
43   Matanga, a Vedantist philosopher of the 13th century.
44   H. Sauvageot, "India Today"; Cahiers du Sud, 1949.
45-46   Radhesyam Purohit, "Indian Classical Music," The New Musical Journal, February, 1962.
47   René Daumal, "India's Real Message"; Cahiers du Sud, 1949.
48   "Looking at India"; Cahiers du Sud, 1941.
49   Encyclopedia of the Pleiades.
50-51   Will Durant, op. cit.
52   Srinivasa Aiyanger, op. cit.
53   For details of these styles, see article cited above by Radhesyam Purohit.
54   See the analysis of the gamelan in the Encyclopedia of the Pleiades.
55-57   M. Granet, Chinese Thought; Albin Michel, 1950.
58   Encyclopedia of the Pleiades.
59   M. Granet, op. cit.
60   Swiss Musical Review, March, 1948.
61   "Keisi Sakka," Musica, September, 1960.
62   Emile Mireaux, Life in the Time of Homer; Hachette.
63-64   Cited by R. Flaceliere, Greece in the Time of Pericles; Hachette, 1959.
65   Ottavio Tiby, Encyclopedia of the Pleiades.
66-67   R. Flaceliere, op. cit.
68   The Foundations of Music in the Human Conscience; La Baconniere.
69   Alfred Einstein, History of Music.

Suggested List of Records

For the reader who wishes to recapture the actual sound of primitive music, there are a number of recordings made in Africa and Australia. Unfortunately, however, it is not always easy to verify their scientific authenticity.

Many recordings of traditional Oriental music are also available.

The following list is by no means exhaustive; it is intended merely as a guide to the reader in his choice of specialized recordings.

AFRICA

A wide choice of African tribal music is given by Folkways, a company specializing in folklore and ethnological recordings:

Africa—Belgian Congo
Africa—British East
Africa—Bulu of the Cameroons
Africa—Central
Africa Coast Rhythms
Africa—Dahomey
Africa—Drums
Africa—French Equatorial
Africa—Manlinke and Baoule
Africa—Music of the Baoule
Africa—Nigeria (Drums of Yoreba)
Africa—Pygmies of the Ituri Forest
Africa—Senegal
Africa—South of the Sahara
Watutsi Songs of Ruanda, etc.

The following records are available from Ariola (Eurodisc):

Africa Dances and Sings
(Choice made by R. Italiaander)

Christophorus:

Makadanganga (songs from the Congo and dances from East Africa)
(Recordings made under the direction of Boris Konictzko)

Columbia:

Bantu Folk Music

AUSTRALIA

RCA Victor:
   The Land of the Morning Star
   (Australia and New Guinea)
Columbia:
   Aboriginal Music—New Guinea
   (edited by Prof. Elkin)
Folkways:
   Tribal Music

EAST AND MIDDLE EAST

Angel:
   Music of India (several records)
Bruno:
   Central Asia: Kirghiz and Kazaks
   Tadjikistan
Barenreiter-Valois (Unesco collection):
   India
   Tibet I, II, and III
   Laos
   Cambodia
   Afghanistan
   Iran I, II, etc.
Chant du Monde:
   Indonesian Gamelans
Columbia:
   Dancers of Bali
   Azuma Kabuki Musicians (Japan)
   Sounds of India
   Japan: Folk Music
   Indonesia (edited by Japp Kunst)
Counterpoint (Vogue):
   Music from Bali (Pierre Ivanoff expedition)
   Music from Borneo   "   "   "
Evergreen:
   Afghanistan and Iran
Folkways:
   Iran and Iraq
   Buddhist Chants and Hymns
   India—Ragas
   India—Religious Music

India—Classic Music
Indonesia
Japan
Japan—Buddhist Ritual
Thailand
Korea
Pakistan
China: Classic Instrumental Music
Guilde Internationale du Disque:
Songs and Dances of Korea
Music from Asia
Lyrichord:
Tsai-ping Liang Instr. Group:
China's Instrumental Heritage
Thrift Edition (Period Consiton):
Music of the Japanese Imperial Court
Music from the Buddhist Temples
Old Chinese Music
Bali
Borneo
Westminster:
Balinese Gamelan (several records)
World:
Shankar, Ravi-India's Master Musician
Japan: Eto, Kimio-Koto
Koto and Flute

ALASKA

Folkways:
Eskimo Music of Alaska and Hudson Bay

ARABIAN MUSIC

Folkways:
Arabic and druse music
Music of Aouth Arabia
Westminster:
Music from Morocco
Songs from Yemen, Atlas Mts., Tunisia

ISRAEL

Schwann:
    Music from Biblical Times: Ancient He-
    brew Melodies (edited by Edith Gerson-
    Kiwi)
Supraphon:
    Jewish Religious Songs
    Synagogal Songs

EGYPT

Telefunken:
    Egyptian Folk Music (recordings made
    under the direction of Charles Gregoire,
    Duke of Mecklembourg)

170

170   Wooden rhombus. (New Guinea)
171   Flat wooden drum. (New Hebrides Islands, Pacific Ocean)

171

Acknowledgments

Thanks are due to all those people and organizations that have made this work possible, especially to: Suzanne Patrick; Renate Wulff; Roger Ségalat; Wolf Strobel; Claus Hansmann; Hans Ulrich Kerth; The National Conservatory of Music, Paris; The Collection of Musical Instruments in the City Museum, Munich; The Museum of Mankind, Paris; and The Ethnological Museum, Munich.

The illustrations come from the following public and private collections:

The National Library, Paris—figures 13, 16, 21, 24, 36, 46-49, 52, 61, 62, 72, 79-86, 88-94, 101, 107, 108, 113-116, 133, 135-146, 153, 154, 159-165, 172 and figures not numbered in the Suggested List of Records.

Library and Museum of Decorative Arts, Paris—fig. 22, 23, 57-60, 63-65, 99, 134, 157, 158.

National Conservatory of Music, Paris—fig. 104, 105, 111.

Museum of Mankind, Paris—fig. 1, 2, 4, 5, 7, 8, 10, 54-56, 106, 112, 170, 171.

Collection of Antiquities, Munich—fig. 149-152.

Ethnological Museum, Munich—fig. 73, 102.

Puppet Theatre Collection, City Museum, Munich—fig. 66.

City Museum, Munich—fig. 6, 42, 67-71, 74-78, 103, 121, 122, 126, 127, 130, 169.

British Museum, London—fig. 32.

Victoria and Albert Museum, London—fig. 50.

Israel Department of Antiquities—fig. 14.

Photographic Archives, Paris—fig. 37, 39, 41, 43, 44, 51, 109, 110.

Boudot-Lamotte, Paris—fig. 27-29, 33, 38, 155, 156.

Giraudon, Paris—fig. 9, 45, 148.

Sirot, Paris—fig. 11.

Viollet, Paris—fig. 40, 147.

Braunmuller, Munich—fig. 87.

Egger, Cologne—fig. 12.

Hansmann, Munich—fig. 17-20, 117-120, 123-125, 128, 129, 131, 132.

Bouvier, Geneva—fig. 166-168.

Private Collection—fig. 3, 53, 100.

172 *Chinese drum. (18th century)*